DREAMS

IN THE SAME SERIES...

Principles of Acupuncture
Angela Hicks
Principles of Aromatherapy
Cathy Hopkins
Principles of Art Therapies
Daniel Brown
Principles of Buddhism
Kulananda
Principles of Chinese Herbal Medicine
John Hicks
Principles of Chinese Medicine
Angela Hicks
Principles of Colonic Irrigation
Jillie Collings
Principles of Colour Healing
Ambike Wauters and Gerry Thompson
Principles of the Enneagram
Karen Webb
Principles of Fasting
Leon Chaitow
Principles of Feng Shui
Simon Brown
Principles of Hypnotherapy
Vera Peiffer
Principles of Jungian Spirituality
Vivianne Crowley
Principles of Kinesiology
Maggie La Tourelle and Anthea Courtenay
Principles of Meditation
Christina Feldman
Principles of Native American Spirituality
Dennis Renault and Timothy Freke
Principles of NLP
Joseph O'Connor and Ian McDermott
Principles of Numerology
Sonia Ducie
Principles of Nutritional Therapy
Linda Lazarides
Principles of Paganism
Vivienne Crowley
Principles of Palmistry
Lilian Verner-Bonds
Principles of Past Life Therapy
Judy Hall
Principles of your Psychic Potential
David Lawson
Principles of Psychotherapy
Brice Avery
Principles of Reflexology
Nicola Hall
Principles of Reiki
Kajsa Krishni Boräng
Principles of Self-Healing
David Lawson
Principles of Shamanism
Leo Rutherford
Principles of Shiatsu
Chris Jarmey
Principles of Stress Management
Vera Peiffer
Principles of Tai Chi
Paul Brecher
Principles of Tarot
Evelyne and Terry Donaldson
Principles of Vibrational Healing
Clare Harvey and Amanda Cochrane
Principles of Wicca
Vivianne Crowley
Principles of Yoga
Cheryl Isaacson

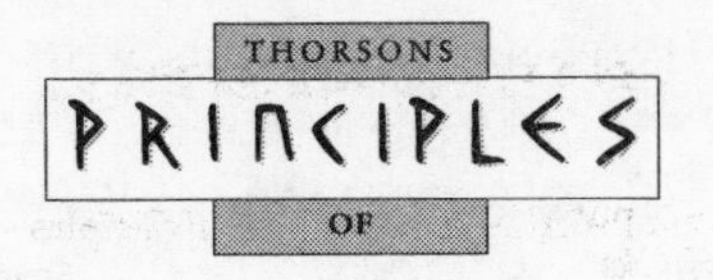

DREAMS

SOOZI HOLBECHE

Thorsons
An Imprint of HarperCollins*Publishers*

'AS I LIVE AND AM A MAN, THIS IS AN UNEXAGGERATED TALE – MY DREAMS BECOME THE SUBSTANCES OF MY LIFE.'
S. T. COLERIDGE

WITH LOVE FOR MAGGIE ROBERTS. MAY ALL YOUR BEST DREAMS COME TRUE, MAY THEY TOO BECOME 'THE SUBSTANCES OF [YOUR] LIFE'.

Thorsons
An Imprint of HarperCollins*Publishers*
77–85 Fulham Palace Road,
Hammersmith, London W6 8JB

Published by Thorsons 1998
3 5 7 9 10 8 6 4

A catalogue record for this book
is available from the British Library

ISBN 0 7225 3548 1

Printed and bound in Great Britain by
Caledonian International Book Manufacturing Ltd, Glasgow

CONTENTS

INTRODUCTION

Since the dawn of time dreams have fascinated mankind. Dreams from the Bible, mystics, shamans and wise men, poets, authors, artists, scientists and psychologists have been a source of creativity and knowledge crucial to the development of civilization.

Ancient scripts and scrolls provide us with dreams and their interpretations that date back thousands of years. Clay tablets have been discovered, inscribed with dreams from Babylon and Assyria, dating from around 3000 BC. The Indian *Vedas*, written around 1000 BC, the Egyptian *Papyrus of Deral-Madineh*, dated 2000 BC, and the Chinese *Meno Shu*, dated about AD 640, all describe dream messages and how to procure them. The Roman soothsayer Artemidorous wrote a book on dreams, the *Oneirocritica*, in the second century AD, which had a profound effect on all subsequent dream research. Aristotle described dreams as 'uncontrolled little eddies formed in rivers…' and also said that 'the most skilful interpreter of dreams is he who has the faculty of observing resemblances…'

In Greek mythology the god of sleep, Hypnos, and the god of death, Thanatos, are twins representing two sides of the condition. Homer, the Greek writer and philosopher, described the 'Gates of Ivory and Horn' through which dreams came.

Dreams that were 'true and good' passed through the Gate of Horn, while dreams that 'deceived or deluded' passed through the Ivory Gate.

In AD 332 Alexander the Great had a dream which caused him to believe that if he laid siege to the city of Tyre he would win it. Encouraged by his dream, he fought and won. St Francis of Assisi was also encouraged by a dream. During arguments with the Pope, he dreamed that he grew enormously tall. This image gave him the courage to continue his fight and found his own religious order – the Franciscans. St Joan of Arc's dreams stimulated her to fight for France against the English. Some dreams have not been so propitious. Before his assassination, Abraham Lincoln dreamed of a coffin surrounded by weeping people and guarded by soldiers. 'Who is dead?' he asked. 'The President. Killed by an assassin,' was the reply. The assassination of President Kennedy was also predicted in many dreams, including those of a woman who telephoned the White House the day before and warned that if Kennedy went to Dallas he would die.

Biblical dreams were believed to be direct messages from God. Examples of these include those in which Joseph saw an angel, Jacob's dream of angels climbing a ladder to heaven; and the vision of another Joseph, who dreamed he and his brothers were binding sheaves of corn in a field and his stood upright while his brothers' sheaves bowed in obeisance.

Other views on dreams were somewhat different. In 1726 Defoe wrote, 'To dream is nothing else but to think sleeping,' while according to the Jewish Talmud 'A dream which is not understood is like a letter which is unopened.'

Shakespeare mentions dreams in most of his plays, to the extent that he used the word 'dream' 150 times altogether. One of his most famous quotes, voiced by Prospero in *The Tempest*, is: 'We are such stuff as dreams are made on,' while Mercutio, in *Romeo and Juliet*, said, 'True, I talk of dreams; which are the children of an idle brain begot of nothing but fantasy.' Romeo himself dreamed 'My lady came and found me dead ... and breathed such life with kisses on my lips that I revived and was an emperor...'

Thomas de Quincey, an opium addict, described dreams in which he was kissed with cancerous kisses by crocodiles, and 'stared at, hooted at, grinned at, chattered at, by monkeys, by parakeets, by cockatoos. Thousands of years I lived and was buried in stone coffins, with mummies and sphinxes'. A similar opium-induced sleep brought the poet Coleridge his famous 'Kubla Khan' poem which begins 'In Xanadu did Kubla Khan a stately pleasure-dome decree ...' A few years ago, while doing research for another book, I discovered that Kubla Khan himself supposedly built his temple as the result of his dreams.

Opium is not necessary for creative dreaming, however, as Charlotte Brontë proved. In *Villette* her description of opium addiction was so exact that she was asked by Mrs Gaskell, who wrote her biography, if she had ever taken it. Brontë said, 'No,' but went on to describe how she thought intently about a subject for a possible book before sleep and literally dreamed herself into the character or experience she wanted to write about. In the morning she awoke with total, seemingly experiential, knowledge of her subject.

The novelist Robert Louis Stevenson had slightly different ways of using dreams. His 'Dream Brownies' generated his short stories and even supplied him with the inspiration for *The Strange Case of Dr Jekyll and Mr Hyde*. Similarly, J. W. Dunne's precognitive dreams led him to write *An Experiment with Time*, in which he suggests that what we consider 'now' is also partly in the past and partly in the future. More recently, Kekule, the German chemist, discovered the molecular structure of benzene through his dreams. When he reported his findings at a conference he said, 'Let us learn to dream, gentlemen, then we may perhaps find the truth.' Elias Howe had already done just that, completing his invention of the sewing-machine as a direct result of dreaming the solution to a problem apparently unsolvable by his waking mind. As to how all this could happen, Henry David Thoreau suggested an answer when he wrote, 'In dreams we see ourselves naked and acting out our real characters, even more clearly than we see others awake,' while for Jung, the great psychiatrist who did a lot of work on dreaming, dream was 'a little hidden door in the innermost and most secret recesses of the psyche'.

During the twentieth century psychological studies of dreaming, together with sleep laboratories and brain research institutes, have become increasingly popular, and dreamwork has become an important part of psychological analysis. Books, seminars, television and radio programmes have all helped to move many people away from the assumption that dreams are 'only your imagination' or 'too much cheese for supper' and brought about the awareness that dreams have altered the fates of entire cultures and shaped the destinies of thousands of individuals.

Dreams teach, balance, inspire and heal not only the world's most original and creative thinkers, but everyone else too. Ever since I was a child dreams have played a vital role in my own life and empowered me to do many things I would not otherwise have dreamed of doing. A dream got me back on my feet after an illness that led to a near-death experience, and another dream helped me to recover from an accident in which I smashed my face into the corner of a steel-capped trunk. Dreams have stimulated my mind, answered my questions and nudged me to recognize right from wrong.

As we move towards the next millennium, thousands of people are seeking to know more about themselves, life in general and the future in particular. Is the road ahead one of cataclysmic change or peace, harmony and brotherly love? Should I take this job/leave my lover/move to another country? How can I solve the problem with my in-laws? The next door neighbour's dog/my new invention? Did I know XYZ in another life? How can I improve my wealth/health/happiness?

This book is an attempt to share with you how the understanding of dreams and dream power can help answer these questions and enable each one of us to find meaning, purpose and fulfilment in our lives.

WHAT EXACTLY ARE DREAMS?

> 'We are such stuff as dreams are made on; and our little life is rounded with a sleep.'
>
> WILLIAM SHAKESPEARE, THE TEMPEST

The Penguin Dictionary of Psychology describes a dream as a 'train of hallucinatory experiences with a certain degree of coherence, but often confused and bizarre, taking place in the condition of sleep and similar conditions'. This is but one of the latest attempts to define the mysterious world of dreams. In ancient times dreams were revered as messages from the soul, gifts from God. According to Job, in the Bible (33:14):

> 'In a dream, in a vision of the night, when sleep falleth upon men in slumberings upon the bed; then He openeth the ears of men, and speaketh their instructions, that He may withdraw man from his purpose and hide pride from man.'

Yet neither Cicero the Roman orator nor the Greek philosopher Aristotle, who were born 300 years apart, would have agreed that the source of a dream was God or the gods. Aristotle wrote that dreams were 'perceptions of sensory-based occurrences' and Cicero described them as:

'phantoms and apparitions ... There is no imaginable thing too absurd, too involved, or too abnormal for us to dream about... Do the immortal gods, who are of surprising excellence in all things, constantly flit about, not only the beds, but even the lowly pallets of mortals...and when they find him snoring, throw at him dark and twisted visions... or does nature bring it to pass that the very active soul sees in sleep phantoms of what it saw when the body was awake?'

Modern dream research shows that both Cicero and Aristotle were partly right in their definition of dreams. However, only *partly* right, because there is also a spiritual dimension to dreaming that I will come on to later.

Certainly dreams mirror the day's events, review unresolved problems, help identify and analyse emotional undercurrents we may not have been fully aware of, and bring to the surface of our minds unconscious desires, conflicts and impulses. Our dream figures may sometimes appear like 'phantoms and apparitions' because they exist in a different reality, beyond time and space, and have the freedom to act, react and change in infinitely different ways that are impossible in waking life. In fact, dreams generally display a range of creativity and intelligence that most of us could not achieve even if we were to remain awake 100 years or more.

So, dreams can heal, teach, warn and guide us. They can also answer questions, connect us to the past, present and future, provide us with amusement and pleasure, bring emotional balance, stimulate creativity and sexuality, solve problems, prepare us for the unknown and enable us to live out unlived parts of ourselves. When Jung talked about the prophetic aspect of dreams, he said that some dreams, as well as visions and thoughts, can suddenly appear, and however carefully these are explored, the cause remains elusive: 'Sometimes an external event can explain the dream or it may be a prognosis of the future ... only our conscious does not know, our unconscious (guided by instinct) does.'

Dreams reveal our own personal mythology, which is the base from where we perceive and experience the world around us. A myth is a pattern of thought or belief, and our personal myths are formed from our temperament, beliefs and attitudes inherited from our parents and the social climate and culture in which we grow up. Joseph Campbell described myths as public dreams and dreams as private myths. A psychiatrist friend describes personal myths as 'the lens through which the human psyche perceives and organizes reality'. These myths can cause unconscious patterns of behaviour towards ourselves, others and the world in general, that stifle our joy, freedom and creativity, and listening to and then acting on our dreams' wisdom can help us overcome our old beliefs and negative attitudes.

So dreams can be thought of as a language, the language of the night, internal communications between myriad aspects of ourselves; a bridge between mind and body, body and spirit, conscious and unconscious. Dreams connect us to a superior source of intelligence that is wise, honest and emotionally detached from our waking selves. This intelligence is the voice of the soul – if we listen to it, it will transform our lives.

Paul Solomon, the American spiritual healer, teacher and mystic, found this out literally when he had his first psychic breakthrough during a sleep-like trance. A voice spoke through him and instructed him on how to improve the quality of his life. When it was asked who or what it was, it replied, 'I am the source of Paul's intelligence, a part of Paul's consciousness that knows everything from the beginning of time.' When asked if this intelligence was unique to Paul, because he was a genius, the answer was a firm 'No. This intelligence is available to every single human being, but most are either unaware of it or are unable to contact it.' Having worked with Paul for many years, I now realize that dreams provide one of the safest, simplest ways of contacting this intelligence – of being in touch with one's own inner guide.

The connection is expressed in dreams through their mix of conscious and unconscious events, their translation of feelings, thoughts and words into pictures, symbols and metaphors. The word 'metaphor', which is a figure of speech, comes from the Greek *meta*, meaning 'over' and *pherin*, 'to carry on'. A metaphor carries one thing over from another and puts images on words or feelings, concepts and events. In *Man and his Symbols*, Jung said that a metaphor affects us on three levels: mental, emotional and imaginative: 'The metaphor's simultaneous operation on these three levels enables the metaphor to make a deep connection with the psyche.' Marion Woodman, the well-known Jungian analyst, says, 'If a metaphor really hits you, it gives you goose pimples.'

Dream images can certainly do this. They are rich, colourful and explicit, and sometimes appear so completely real we believe that what we saw in a dream actually happened in life. In the early 1900s, for example, a French newspaper described a Parisian man who dreamed he had murdered his wife and two daughters. Distraught, he rushed from his bed to the local gendarmerie and confessed his crime. When the gendarme went to investigate, he found the man's wife and daughters sitting round the table having breakfast.

D. H. Lawrence found dreams so real that, in a letter to a friend, he wrote:

> 'I can never decide whether my dreams are the result of my thoughts, or my thoughts the result of my dreams. It is very queer but my dreams make conclusions for me. They decide things finally. I dream a decision. Sleep seems to hammer out for me

> the logical conclusion of my vague days and offer me them as dreams.'

Dreams *will* give us signs, reminders and warnings that may help us choose one path or another, but will never make the choice for us, even if it seemed to Lawrence that 'dreams make conclusions for me'. The objective and honest insight dreams give us, if we listen to them, *can* result in our waking up with a totally clear answer to what may have been, pre-sleep, an insoluble situation or problem. However, a dream, like any other form of spiritual guidance, will never *decide* for us.

According to Paul Solomon's source, dreams are 'acts of the soul that assess how we handle the lessons of the day'. These assessments are then recorded on the Akashic records – the record of everything that has ever happened since the beginning of time, similar to Jung's 'collective unconscious' – and reflected back to our conscious mind through dreams. In other words, dreams are like mirrors that show us exactly where we are in life and what we need to know about ourselves.

During the years I spent with Paul in America I discovered a number of extraordinary spiritual teachers, wise men and women who encouraged me to listen to my heart and, despite strong opposition from my family, to follow the path my feet were now on. One of these was the amazingly wise and intuitively gifted Ann Ree Colton, who is described on the cover of her book *Watch Your Dreams* as a 'prophet, clairvoyant and teacher of teachers'. For over 50 years Ann Ree Colton interpreted thousands of dreams and made many dreamers aware of what she called 'the Night Ministry'. By this she meant that during sleep we can study in universities known as Halls of Learning, learn about past lives, explore the future and help others if we wish. In the course of her work, Ann Ree Colton observed the difference between what she called 'lower psychic'

or 'astral level' dreams, spiritually instructive dreams, and archetypal 'drama and myth' type dreams. (An archetype is a spontaneously recurring pattern within the collective psyche, or unconscious, of all mankind). In Colton's own words:

> 'Dreams may be projected from the depths of the lower mind or from the heights of one's higher or eternal self ... Dreams may stir one's lesser (instinctive) emotions, causing unrest and fear, or they may fill one with blessed peace ...'

Ann Ree Colton also found a sequential pattern in dreams which she saw reflected in a person's progress through life.

Jung too, discovered that dreams seemed to follow an arrangement or pattern. He called this 'the process of individuation', i.e. the process of discovering the true self. Jung estimated that during his life he interpreted at least 80,000 dreams. He discovered that dreams were not only relevant to the dreamer but were also part of 'a great web of psychological factors' and 'the subliminal picture of the psychological condition of the individual in his waking state ...'

While Jung examined dreams for what they might reveal, his early mentor Freud looked for what they might conceal. Freud also believed that sleep was restorative and a dream was a compromise between a person's need for expression and a need for rest. Therefore he sometimes called dreams the 'guardians of sleep' as well as the 'Royal Road to understanding the unconscious'. Both Freud and Jung have had a profound effect on our attitude to our dreams today and their dreamwork has coloured the world of modern psychology.

Taking some steps along Freud's Royal Road could broaden our horizons immeasurably. The eminent psychologist William James once said that most people live in a very restricted circle of their potential being and make very little use of the resources, especially the soul's resources, available to them. He likened this to a man who, with an entire body available to explore and enjoy, only moved the little finger of one hand. James said, 'We all have reservoirs of life to draw upon of which we do not dream'. But it is through dreams that we can tap into vast reservoirs of intelligence, memory and creativity that can empower us all to master life's challenges, instead of feeling victimized by them.

THE POWER OF SLEEP

Some say that gleams of a remoter world visit the soul in sleep.

DANTE

'To sleep; perchance to dream,' so runs Hamlet's refrain, yet how many of us dismiss both sleep and dreaming as unimportant. However, as Samuel Johnson observed in 1758, sleep is 'a state in which a great part of every life is passed'. In fact, during an average lifetime we spend approximately 24 years asleep and six of those years dreaming. These six years are longer than the average college or university course, but most of us just throw this time away.

Sleep was not always so lightly dismissed, however. Early esoteric schools in which students were initiated into the 'mysteries' – sometimes known as Mystery Schools or Schools of Wisdom – taught that it was a magical time, an opportunity for the soul to leave the body and commune with the gods. It was revered as a period in which to learn, take stock and explore other worlds. Sleep was also considered a preparation for death because in both sleep and death, the spirit withdraws from physical consciousness and is not extinguished.

Following on from this idea, communities such as the Essenes, to which Joseph and Mary, the parents of Jesus, belonged, believed that preparation for sleep was as vital as preparation for death. Sleep was for them a 'little death'. Each day was greeted as a new birth, a new life, and at the end of the day, before the sun set, quarrels and arguments were resolved. Any person in need of forgiveness was forgiven. Before sleep, the day's events were reviewed, acknowledged and released. In the words of the Dead Sea Scrolls, 'When the sun is set and your Heavenly Father sends you his most precious angel, Sleep, then take your rest and be all night with the Angel of Sleep...'

While, for many people in the past sleep was a mystical experience, for many people today, however, it is a form of anaesthesia, an escape from life and its problems. So, desperate for sleep, we swallow pills or drown ourselves in alcohol or sex.

Sleep is, in effect, an altered state of consciousness and for hundreds of years it has been the source of much speculation. Questions such as what was the purpose of sleep, what happened to the brain during sleep, and was sleep caused by the relaxation of certain glands, muscles and organs have long taxed the minds of scientists, wise men and philosophers.

Nineteenth-century research suggested that 'poisonous substances' formed in the body during the day were only eliminated during sleep. Maybe these early researchers were not far wrong. Dr Stanley Krippener, an American clinical psychologist and former director of the Dream Laboratory at the Maimonides hospital in New York, with whom I once worked, says that there is a biochemical substance that accumulates during the day and which can only be released from the nervous system during sleep and dreams. Dr Krippener believes that sleep and dreaming are as necessary to man as eating and drinking: 'Any disturbance that interrupts sleep will interfere with dream-time, thus leaving the individual less well prepared, physically and psychologically, to face the coming day.'

Certainly sleep clinics world-wide have discovered that, after colds, sleep problems are the most common health complaint.

Lack of sleep, especially dream sleep, can lead to mental illness, accidents and carelessness at work. William James went so far as to describe sleep itself as 'a dreadful disease'!

Another American doctor, sleep specialist Dr William Dement, says, 'People who have accumulated a large sleep debt are dangerous on the highway, dangerous in the sky, dangerous wherever they are. That is because an attack of uncontrollable sleepiness is just as unpredictable as an earthquake and maybe just as devastating.' An example of this is the Chernobyl nuclear accident in Russia, which Dement believes was caused by lack of sleep.

Another doctor, Dr Moore-Ede, who has worked with hundreds of nightshift workers in different companies all over the world, says that nearly 80 per cent of them nod off at some point during the night, or reach a point of drowsiness that causes them to make mistakes. Moore-Ede's research concludes that even if we miss two hours sleep in one night, we are sleep deprived and, in experiments with rats, sleep deprivation actually caused death.

A few years ago I worked briefly with Dr Stanley Krippener. As part of his dream research I watched volunteer sleepers being woken four or five times a night in mid-dream sleep. After a few days of this treatment the sleepers became confused, irritable and emotionally unstable. Some even developed panic attacks and refused to continue the programme. When the same group was woken during non-dream sleep they were tired but not upset. So I saw for myself that it is not sleep but *dream* deprivation that is so harmful. Dr Krippener's research also showed that alcohol, sleeping pills and amphetamines depress dream time but coffee does not. (I find the latter statement hard to accept, though, because if I drink coffee in the evening I do not sleep and therefore do not dream!)

Research into the relationship between body, mind, brain and sleep began hundreds of years ago. However, it was not until

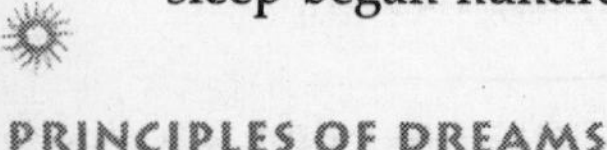

the physics of electricity was understood and EEG (electroencephalogram) instruments, which amplify brain voltage, were invented, that scientists began to understand how the brain works.

In 1952, EEGs enabled two researchers, Nathaniel Kleitman, a physiologist and sleep scientist at the University of Chicago, and Eugene Aserinsky, a graduate student working in Kleitman's laboratory, to make a breakthrough in sleep research. The EEGs showed them that during sleep the brain had periods of activity as intense as when its owner was awake. This demolished the theory that the sleeping brain was simply resting.

J. Allan Hobson, author of *The Dreaming Brain*, describes the brain as a 'chatterbox – an enormously complex information-processing machine ... the number of its elements greater than the population of the world with virtually instantaneous communication from cell to cell'. He likens it to 20 billion citizens talking to some 10,000 others at least once and sometimes even 100 times a second. During dreams, Hobson says, it's as if 'the brain literally talks to itself'.

Through EEGs Kleitman and Aserinsky discovered the connection between brain activity, rapid eye movement, now known as REM, and dreaming. They saw that REM occurred during dream sleep but not during non-dream or slow wave sleep. They also found that most people woken during REM sleep remembered their dreams in detail, while those left to sleep without interruption usually had no dream recall whatsoever.

Today we know that REM sleep, or dreaming, begins about 90 minutes after we fall asleep and will re-occur every 90 minutes, approximately four or five times a night. Newborn babies spend much of their sleeping time in REM, which many doctors believe is essential for their brain development. As we get older, our need for REM sleep diminishes and we dream less.

Our brainwave rhythms, sometimes called 'frequencies' or 'cycles', also change during different phases of sleep. These rhythms are named after letters in the Greek alphabet: beta, alpha, theta and delta. Beta is the active, assessing, decision-making part of the brain which we use when awake. Alpha is a slower, more receptive rhythm, which we can drift into, with our eyes open or closed, when we relax. Movies, television, music, visualization, deep breathing, yoga, massage, anything that induces deep relaxation can put us into alpha. Theta frequencies are slower still and it is usually when alpha reaches its lowest vibrational frequency and moves into theta that real dreaming starts. Delta is the slowest cycle of all and occurs in profound sleep under anaesthetic or in the womb. Sleep comes when our brain's mind moves from beta to alpha to theta to delta. In Sri Lanka, where I was born, I have watched yogis who can induce delta at will. They learn to do this as part of a spiritual discipline which enables them to control their heartbeat, respiration and nervous system. Consciously using delta, they can walk through pits of fire, pierce their limbs with nails and long knives and lie buried in the earth for days at a time. I never saw any physical damage, such as burns or bleeding afterwards.

In the West most of us spend our entire waking lives using only the beta brainwave. We are either unaware of, or ignore, the alpha, theta and delta levels. This means that we use only 10 per cent of our brain capacity, while 90 per cent remains submerged, like part of an iceberg. As soon as we begin to listen to our dreams, ask questions of them, and act on the answers and information given to us, however, we immediately draw on far more of our intelligence than before. This can empower us to do, change or become, anything we want. This is especially important if we want to change addictive patterns of behaviour, most of which are based on survival strategies learned in childhood.

For example, Pauline excelled at school while her adopted brother Alistair lagged behind. Yet Pauline's parents never once praised Pauline for her success, but constantly admired Alistair for his limited efforts. To gain her parents' approval Pauline began to fail exams she could easily have passed. This led to an unconscious belief that success meant lack of love and recognition, while failure stimulated love and approval. This belief set in motion a pattern in Pauline's adult life where each time she was on the verge of success, whether in work or a relationship, she either failed or opted out. Once she realized this, she decided to use dreams to help overcome her problem.

Pauline asked for dreams to heal and empower her. During a six-month series of dreams she saw herself as if on a movie screen as a disappointed child who yearned for encouragement but never got it. A voice said, 'It is now your responsibility to take care of this child.' In one dream she saw herself caring for an abandoned baby she found in a lift that zoomed to the top floor of a skyscraper building in New York; in another she pushed a baby out of its pram and took its place. Probably the most important dream was one in which her parents, long dead, appeared and said; 'We are truly sorry for any pain we caused. You were always so brilliant and we did not want Alistair to feel left out, so we praised him, hoping he would try to achieve what you did. We loved you so much, we did not want him to feel we loved him less.' By drawing on the power, perception and energy of her dreaming mind, Pauline overcame her block and became a happy and successful woman.

Pauline actualized her dreams, which simply means she acted on, or used in her waking life, the information she gained during the night. When we do this, the 90 per cent alpha, theta and delta frequencies co-operate with us rather than unconsciously fighting us.

When we make the decision to go to bed, our brainwave rhythm is beta. As we relax and drift into a half-awake, half-asleep state, we lower this rhythm to alpha. It is now that hypnagogic images may appear. These images are normally very clear and can include faces, landscapes, animals, dots, stars, flowers or even geometric shapes and blobs of colour. In 1861 Alfred Maury, a French scientist, described experiments in which he found he could trigger all sorts of hypnagogic imagery by pressing his own eyeballs. In one image a blob of light turned into a maid in a white uniform, who then spoke and told him she had cleaned his room. Maury went on to introduce methods of pre-sleep stimuli to trigger hypnagogic images which he hoped would continue into the subsequent dreams of the night.

Like Maury, Hervey St Denis, a French aristocrat, was fascinated by hypnagogic images. In 1867 he wrote a book called *Dreams and How to Control Them* in which he described one of his own:

> 'A crystal green colour takes shape in the centre of my internal visual field. I make out little by little that it is a collection of leaves. It boils, like a volcano about to erupt, it swells and expands rapidly. Red flowers come out of the crater and make an enormous bouquet … then it all evaporates.'

We can stimulate hypnagogic images for ourselves by copying Maury and pressing our own eyelids gently with our fingertips or by looking at brightly coloured pictures before going to sleep. Some researchers describe them as hallucinations. However, they are not the hallucinations of madness, but simply a normal part of the brain shifting gear from one level to another. While some of us have such 'hallucinations' when we drift into sleep, and others when we wake up, no one appears to have them every night.

The early alpha stage of sleep, during which these hypnagogic images may appear, is so light that we may easily wake during it and insist we have not been asleep. We gradually enter a deeper phase which brings overall relaxation, a slower heart rate, a drop in blood pressure and temperature. About 90 minutes after falling asleep we move into our first dream phase and continue throughout the night to drift between deep, restorative sleep and spectacular, revelatory dream periods.

The most spectacular revelatory dreamer of all time was undoubtedly the American Edgar Cayce, who became known as 'the Sleeping Prophet'. While asleep he could diagnose illness, outline medical treatments he had never heard of and correctly describe people he had never seen, even if they were hundreds of miles away. Edgar Cayce practised medical diagnosis by clairvoyance for 43 years. By the time he died in 1945, he had gathered together 30,000 diagnostic reports and hundreds of complete case reports containing affidavits and testimonies from patients and doctors that confirmed the accuracy of his treatment.

Edgar Cayce discovered his gifts when, as a young man, a hypnotist at a local fair put him into a deep sleep in an attempt to cure his paralysed vocal chords, which had prevented him from speaking. Suddenly, while asleep, Cayce spoke. He diagnosed the cause of his condition and described how to cure it. Later he was able to induce this sleep/trance-like state for himself. Cayce was an extraordinary example of how we can use sleep to delve into the unconscious and super or higher conscious minds.

Paul Solomon, the psychic and healer, had a very similar experience to Cayce's in that his breakthrough into other levels of consciousness came initially through hypnotism, which induced a similar, deep sleep/trance-like state. He too later learned to put himself into a semi-conscious sleep state at will and gave

hundreds of readings (which today would be called channellings) on subjects that ranged from health to spiritual advice and vocational guidance. One of Paul's initial readings was for the parents of a six-week old baby suffering from such chronic digestive problems that the doctors gave him only days, if not hours, to live. Asleep, Paul said the baby must be fed crushed crackers (water biscuits) and pure undiluted Coca-Cola (not the fizzy drink but its base, which originally contained cocaine). Shocked at such a prescription for a virtually newborn baby already at death's door from digestive problems, the parents nevertheless followed Paul's advice. The baby completely recovered.

Years before Mesmer discovered hypnosis, similar results were obtained by a Frenchman, Armand Marc Jacques de Castenet, who used what he called 'magnetism' to treat a patient suffering from convulsions. The patient fell asleep and began to speak with apparent clairvoyant perception and greater intelligence than when awake. Intrigued, de Castenet conducted similar experiments with other patients, all of whom, when asleep, showed the same abilities. In *The Mind of Man*, published in 1937, author Walter Bromberg described de Castenet's work:

> 'Dull peasants became mentally alert and could even foretell events or understand things ordinarily obscure to them. Somnambulists made medical diagnosis in patients brought before them and foretold the future.'

All of these people used sleep as a means to contact a superior intelligence that knew more than their waking selves. This intelligence not only knows more but can also assist us to overcome ordinary everyday problems.

In the words of Byron, 'Our life is two-fold: sleep hath its own world, a boundary between the things misnamed death and

existence: sleep hath its own world, and a wide realm and a wide reality.'

Let us learn to use the wider realm of sleep and dreams to create a new and wonderful world for ourselves.

PREPARING FOR SLEEP

> 'Sleep is so wonderful, it shouldn't be wasted on people too tired to enjoy it.'
>
> ASHLEIGH BRILLIANT

Deep, peaceful sleep is nature's way of recharging our batteries. It is well known to have a curative effect on illness, as it is during sleep that most healing occurs. However, in today's world, stress, anxiety and depression cause thousands of people to suffer from insomnia.

Most of us, whether healthy or sick, just hurl ourselves into bed when we feel tired, without any thought that a little 'sleep preparation' would ensure not only a good night's sleep, but also better dreams. Many of us also suffer sleepless nights through eating and drinking too much too late, so one basic and sensible avenue to good sleep is to eat lightly and less a little earlier in the evening.

Another way to sleep better at night is to leave the day behind. The best method of doing this is to review the day, briefly, before you go to bed. Make notes in a journal or diary, summing up the day as if it were a dream and giving it a title featuring the main event. Briefly think of the chief characters in your day and the emotional impact they had on you and you on them.

Remember that our negative emotional reactions to both people and situations are based on our beliefs about ourselves and about life itself. We tend to think emotions happen to us as the result of another person's actions or attitude. In fact, we can choose whether to react or not if we look at the underlying causes of how we feel. Virtually all the depressing emotions, such as fear, hurt, anger, jealousy, self-pity, guilt, pain, regret and resentment, are caused by a lack of self-love, which results in lack of belief in ourselves. If any such feelings crop up during the day, ask yourself, 'What did I believe about myself in that moment?' and deal with the belief rather than blame anyone else.

If you regret doing something, forgive yourself (and anyone else) for whatever it may be. A simple affirmation of forgiveness that I have used myself for years is: 'The Divine in me forgives the human in me, and in you, for any imbalance, barrier or misunderstanding that has come between us.' Do not carry the events of the day, whether good, bad or indifferent, into the night. Bless them, release them, let them fade from your mind.

If you do not want to write, you can sit with your feet in a bowl of warm water and imagine the day flowing out of your body through your feet and into the water. Take slow, easy breaths as you do so. I find a simple way to breathe and relax is to breathe in through my nose to the count of four, hold the breath to the count of four and sigh the breath out also to the count of four.

You can also take a quartz crystal in either your right or left hand, whichever is most comfortable, mentally sum up the day and breathe it out and into the crystal three times with a sharp *'Hah'* exhaling breath. Then hold the crystal against the centre of your forehead, with your eyes closed, for two to three minutes. The crystal will absorb the day and transmute it, and you will feel a deep peace afterwards.

Another pre-sleep exercise which also clears out the residue of the day's thoughts, feelings and activities is to cleanse one's aura. The aura is an electro-magnetic field made up of a number of subtle or invisible bodies which swirl and move around us, forming a bubble-like shape, which expands when we feel happy and shrinks when we feel depressed. The aura reveals illness before it manifests in our physical bodies, and shows mental and emotional blocks from this and other lives, as well as from our daily experience. Even accidents show up in the aura three to seven days before they happen. It would therefore make sense to have aura-cleansing taught in school as a form of preventative medicine, not just as an aid to better sleep.

There are myriad ways to cleanse and recharge the aura. We can visualize light or colour pouring through the top of our head and expanding outwards to encompass the entire body. We can imagine drawing sunlight into our solar-plexus or diaphragm area and mentally imagine the healing power of the sun revitalizing all our muscles, nerves, organs and glands before we mentally expand it to fill and strengthen the auric bubble around us – as if we had swallowed the sun and the sun had swallowed us. We can also visualize colour and light in spirals around us – clockwise spirals descending and encompassing us from above and anti-clockwise spirals rising up from below our feet.

However, the following method is the one I use every morning when I wake up and every night before I go to bed. If I feel uncomfortable during the day I do it again. I first shake my hands vigorously to recharge their energy. Then, very gently, I touch my middle fingers to the centre of my forehead and brush lightly down the side of my cheeks to under my jaw. I next cup my hands under my chin and lift my linked hands over the top of my head and down to the back of my neck. I make these movements three times. I now put my right hand across and beyond my left shoulder and brush down to my feet, leaving approximately 12" (30cm) between my body and my hand. I repeat the same movement with my left hand down my right side. I next place both hands in the small of my back and brush down over my buttocks and down the back of my legs to the ground. Finally I cup my hands in front of my chest and lift them, with fingertips touching, over my head to the back of my neck, and then bring them forward to brush down the front of my body to my toes and the ground. I ask that anything that is inappropriate to my consciousness may be removed from me. As this is a little like brushing psychic crumbs away, afterwards I always point my fingers to the ground and send any negativity to the light and love of God. I then brush upwards with my hands to recharge and strengthen my aura. You can also do this exercise with crystals. When you have done it a few times, you will notice a dramatic improvement physically, mentally and emotionally.

To induce deep, peaceful sleep we also need to create an atmosphere of tranquility around us. Fresh flowers, crystals, candles, herbs, incense, music, our favourite colours for sheets, pictures and walls can all help our physical senses to surrender to the night. Gems such as amethyst, blue lace agate, moonstone and rose quartz are all helpful for sleep and relaxation. We should try and sleep without clutter and dispose of, or put in another room, anything that does not lift our spirits.

If this is not possible we can always create an *inner* space of peace and harmony. We can imagine the kind of bed or room we would like to sleep in as well as visualize whatever would make us feel really happy. Whether this is the deck of a boat, a log cabin, a tent or a sleeping bag alongside a fast-flowing river or under a tree in a forest, if we practise going there before sleep, our inner space will become so real our bodies will respond as if it exists.

For some of us the position in which our bed is placed –North, West, South or East – can also affect the quality of our sleep. For example, in Native American terms, the power of the North clarifies our mind and thoughts, the power of the West revitalizes and renews our physical bodies and the power of the South stimulates intuition, while the power of the East triggers enlightenment. If we place our bed in different positions through the year, we can discover for ourselves what position and resultant energy suits us best.

Stretching and breathing are important for physical relaxation and physical relaxation is conducive to better sleep. Muscles release tension more easily after a good stretch. Deep breathing assists relaxation and also sends more oxygen to the brain, which helps to clear and relax the mind.

Most of us, unless we practise yoga, or a spiritual discipline that includes breath control, do not breathe properly. The more stressed we become, the more shallow our breathing becomes. We do not understand how the power that comes from correct breathing can transform our lives as well as our sleep.

Breath is *prana*, a Sanskrit word that literally means 'the breath of God'. It refers to the vital energy or creative life force available in the atmosphere around us. It is more than air – it is electricity, magnetism and the energy of God's presence. A simple exercise of conscious breathing is to breath in through the nose the presence of God, love and truth, and exhale through the mouth, pain, imbalance, toxins and tension. Each in-breath should expand the lungs like a bellows. Each out-breath should force the air out with a sound like a groan or a deep sigh. We can do this while sitting in a chair or lying in bed.

Three slightly more energetic breathing exercises I learned from Paul Solomon, who taught them in his Inner Light Consciousness programme. They are simple, effective and work better when used in conjunction with each other. All three combine stretching and breathing and can be used first thing in the morning as well as before sleep and meditation

The first, called 'Climbing to the Light', begins by reaching up as far as you can reach with the left hand and arm. The right heel should come off the floor/ground in your effort to reach and stretch – as if you were trying to pick apples or cherries from a tree whose branches were almost too high to touch. You should feel the stretch diagonally across your body from right heel to left fingers. Inhale sharply as you stretch. Hold the breath – do not exhale. Then do exactly the same with the right arm. Again, inhale more air without exhaling. Now back to the left and then to the right, each time breathing in more air with each upward stretch. This forces air into parts of your body that may never have breathed air into them before. After four stretches – two left, two right – bend forward from the waist and blow the air out. This exercise can be done as many times as you want, but I find it best to repeat the process at least four times for greatest effect.

The second exercise is the 'Sundance Stretch'. For this you need to stand straight and inhale deeply while you raise your left arm slowly to the top of your head. Then lean over far to the right. Hold your breath and bend forward from the waist and sharply exhale. Repeat with the right arm and lean far to the left as you inhale, then again bend forward, bowing to the ground, as you exhale. Repeat both left and right movements four or five times.

'Pulling the Light' is the third exercise. Stand straight, elbows close to your sides, with your fists clenched together at chest level. Breathe in as slowly and deeply as possible. Hold the breath for a moment or two and then punch the breath out sharply five times in rapid succession, while also punching out your fists. Then breathe in sharply five times, filling the lungs more each time, and exhale five times. Co-ordinate the breaths

with five sharp, jerky punctuating in-and-out movements of fists and arms. Try not to hunch your shoulders as you do this.

Do not worry if you feel a little light-headed the first time you perform these exercises. It is simply a sign that you need to practise breathing more deeply than you did before. In fact, if you practise exercises every day – even two or three times a day – you will find you feel so much better you become almost addicted to them.

We all know that relaxation is essential for sound sleep and good health. Stress and tension in the body prevent a clear pre-sleep mind. Stress is the result of our physical and mental reaction to whatever occurs in our lives. Too much stress affects the nervous and immune systems, stimulates an over-production of adrenaline and can break down the chemical balance of the body. Chronic stress can lead to major illness, both mental and physical.

Many of us 'relax' by watching television, having a few glasses of wine, seeing friends, following a sport, or watching a movie. All these activities can help us to switch off, but are not real stress release because even then we have a tendency to control our body, feelings and thoughts. This conscious *and* unconscious need to 'maintain control' leads to tightness and stress in thinking and moving, and blocks inspiration, rest and healing. True relaxation comes if we recognize tension in different parts of the body and take steps to release it. The following exercise will allow both body and mind to let go and drift into a deeply relaxed state. Like the previous stretching and breathing exercises, it will enhance any kind of meditation, visualization or reverie experience, as well as sleep itself.

The first step is to make yourself as comfortable as possible in a place where you will not be disturbed. Wear loose clothes and either lie on the floor with your head on a pillow or sit in a chair that supports your back. (Pre-sleep you can do it in bed.)

Whether you lie down or sit in a chair, place your legs slightly apart and rest your arms a few inches away from your body, with the palms of your hands facing up towards the ceiling.

Close your eyes and take two or three deep breaths in through the nose and out through the mouth, with a really deep *'aagh'* or *'shoo'* exhalation. Throughout the exercise breathe in through the nose and out through the mouth, but without forcing the breath in any way. With every in-breath visualize life force, health, energy and vitality renewing cells, muscles, tissues and organs and the immune, lymphatic, digestive, circulatory and nervous systems of the body. On each out-breath exhale all toxicity, whether from diseased cells, painful memories or present feelings of anger, fear or disappointment.

Continue to breathe easily and peacefully into every part of your body for a minimum of three to five minutes, longer if you have the time. Imagine your body filled with light and/or colour from top to toe, inside and out. Then move your awareness to your left leg. Concentrate on the toes, the sole and arch of the foot, the heel, ankle, calf, shin, knee and thigh. Be aware of any tension. Let your mind and imagination move from toe to thigh and thigh to toe two or three times. Thank your left foot and leg for the support it gives you. (However silly this may sound, to acknowledge, thank and bless different parts of our body helps them to function better. The same applies to any kind of mechanical equipment from car to computer to electric kettle.) Now wiggle your toes, move your ankle, bend your knee, move your leg and thigh and then lift the leg off the floor, point your toes or heel and tense and tighten the leg muscles while you sharply inhale and hold the breath. Then sharply exhale and relax the muscles so that your left leg drops to the floor. Repeat with the right leg. (N.B. It does not matter which leg you do first.)

Now move your awareness to your pelvis, hips, stomach and buttocks. Imagine being inside this area and sense comfort or

discomfort. Thank your spleen, pancreas, gall-bladder, liver, kidneys, colon and bladder for all the work they do. Appreciate the sexual organs for the joy of sex.

Next move your awareness above your diaphragm and solar plexus to your chest, lungs and back. Concentrate on your heart, lungs, ribs and spine. Imagine love for yourself flowing from and to your heart. Then stretch your shoulders back as far as you can to open the lungs and expand the chest. Again, hold your breath and sharply exhale. Now bring your shoulders forward and stretch the back muscles, then hunch your shoulders up towards your ears, tense the muscles, sharply inhale, hold the breath and sharply exhale. Let your shoulders drop and your chest slump.

Next concentrate in turn on your left and right arms. Focus on the fingers, palm, wrist, forearm, elbow and upper arm. Let your imagination move from fingertip to shoulders two or three times. Notice any tension. Then open and close your fingers, bend your wrist and elbow, move your arm and send it love and appreciation. Then straighten and stiffen the arm, and raise it sideways or above your head. Tense and tighten the arm muscles while you sharply inhale, hold your breath then just as sharply exhale and drop your arm.

Now move your attention to your neck and head. Turn your head left and right two or three times. Nod your head forward and back two or three times. Stretch your neck, feel for tension and then roll your head around in a complete circle three times anti-clockwise, three times clockwise. If your neck feels stiff, tap it gently with your fingertips and repeat the stretching and rolling. You should feel a release.

Next concentrate on your head and face. Think of your forehead, eyes, cheeks, ears, jaw, the top and back of your head, your scalp and hair. Appreciate the power of your brain and your senses of smell, sight, hearing and speaking. Then scrunch your eyelids tightly shut and grit your teeth together. Feel and exaggerate the tension. Hold your breath and exhale, still with eyelids tightly shut, then open your mouth as wide as you can – as if you would yawn or scream – and then let go.

Keeping your eyes closed, let yourself sink into the floor, chair or bed. Take a few deep breaths and shuffle or shake your body free from any remaining tension. As you relax, imagine a fountain of sparkling light cascading around and through your body. Make it so real your body tingles. Visualize this light flowing to and through all your muscles, nerves, organs and glands until your entire body glows with light.

This exercise should make you feel as if your body is weightless and you could float away. The more you practise, the greater the results, so do not worry if your initial attempts do not produce immediate and total relaxation.

Meditation, mantras, prayer and music are all aids to sleep and dreams. A mantra is a word, phrase or sound which, when repeated often, causes a physiological change. It focuses the mind on a single point and eliminates extraneous thought, serving in a sense as a 'trigger mechanism' to induce an altered state of consciousness. When the mind is filled with the mantra, thought stops. Repeating a mantra is one of the most effective ways to still and empty the mind before meditation as well as before sleep.

Certain words or sound such as *Elohim*, *I Am*, *Aum* or *Om* have 'mantramic value', which means that the vibratory quality is either relaxing or exciting. Repeating a word or phrase that has mantramic power rhythmically causes the pulse and brainwave rhythms to slow, respiration to ease and tension to be released. It usually takes approximately 20 minutes of chanting or repeating the mantra for this to happen.

Elohim, pronounced 'Ell-o-heem', is a Hebrew name for God meaning 'all that God is'. It is androgynous – in other words it speaks of both feminine and masculine aspects of God. *I Am* is also a universal name for God. *Om* and *Aum* are words long believed to have sacred vibrations. Vowels heal and balance inner consciousness, consonants heal and balance outer consciousness. To combine both consonants and vowels in a mantra is therefore far more powerful.

Ann Ree Colton says that pre-sleep mantras move one 'out of the boundaries of fears and discords of the day, giving winged powers to rise in the night upward in consciousness'.

Prayers have the same effect and prayers spoken aloud, while kneeling, help to expand the heart chakra, as well as the ability to love unconditionally. To pray is to direct one's mind, heart, soul and spirit to the Source of Life. One of my favourite prayers is one I learned in Bulgaria from the teachings of the Bulgarian spiritual teacher Beinsa Douna (sometimes known as Peter Deunov). It runs as follows:

> 'The disciple must have a heart as pure as a crystal,
> A mind as bright as the sun,
> A soul as vast as the universe
> And a spirit as powerful as God and one with God.'
>
> Amen.

An evening prayer also given by Beinsa Douna which creates a good protective vibratory atmosphere around us before sleep is this one:

> 'I thank thee Lord for the experiences of the day,
> Guide me also in the coming night.
> May my soul attend Thy Divine School,
> So that I may learn how to work effectively.'
>
> Amen.

Ann Ree Colton gave this prayer as one that has mantramic power and is especially good before sleep:

'Father let it be Thy will.
Let the past be resolved.
And "let the dead bury their dead".
And in the name of the Lord Christ
May I be instructed, guided and
Enlightened, so that I may better
Seek Thee, discern Thee and Serve Thee.'
Amen.

Ultimately of course, the words we use are far less important than the spirit and genuine feeling behind them. A story about Mahommed illustrates this. Mahommed was walking along a road when he saw a beggar on his knees in the dust. Mahommed asked him what he was doing and the beggar replied, 'I am saying my prayers.' Mahommed said, 'You are not praying correctly. I will teach you.' The beggar was happy to learn the words and ritual that Mahommed taught him and, well pleased with himself, Mahommed went on his way. Suddenly the voice of God spoke, demanding an explanation for his action. When Mahommed answered that he could not stand by and allow the beggar to speak to God improperly, God replied, 'Before, this man spoke from his heart – now he speaks from his head.'

Herbal baths and teas, flower essences, aromatherapy, Aura-Soma oils, foot, hand and face massage, which we can do for ourselves, as well as for each other, are all conducive to relaxation and sleep. Flowers and herbs soothe, heal and feed the spirit. Their subtle vibrations transform us as well as the atmosphere around us.

Out of the many useful and powerful herbal sleep inducers, chamomile, Californian poppy, lime blossom and red clover are

some of the best. A mix of one part valerian and one part passion flower made into a tea and drunk last thing at night releases tension and eases one into sleep.

David Hoffman, author of *The Holistic Herbal*, says that another excellent way to imbibe natural 'nervine relaxants' is through the skin when having a bath. He suggests that this is a particularly good way to help children, as well as adults, sleep better. David's recipe for a valerian bath is to pour one and a half pints (one litre) of boiling water onto one or two handfuls of dried valerian root. Leave it to stand for half an hour, then strain the liquid and add it to a hot bath, which should be taken just before going to bed. This recipe can be used for any of the herbal relaxants.

When I was a child, the Beatrix Potter stories of the Flopsy Bunnies eating lettuce because it had a soporific effect fascinated me. I have no idea what 'soporific' meant but it sounded magical. Today I know that many fruits and vegetables have the same soporific effect as lettuce. In fact any fruit or vegetable high in calcium, magnesium and the B vitamins, especially B6, can help calm the nervous system.

Borage is another herb that strengthens and soothes the nerves and lifts us into peaceful sleep. It can be drunk as a mix with other vegetables or infused as a tea. For the tea, use ¾oz (2gm) of leaves to half a pint (a quarter of a litre) of boiling water or one leaf squeezed into a glass of mixed vegetable juice. Celery and watercress, orange and raspberries, grapefruit and guavas all have a calming effect when taken in a juice before sleep.

Aura-Soma, which combines the Latin word *Aura*, meaning akin to 'air', with *Soma*, which in Sanskrit implies a drink, or 'fragrance', that transports the soul into divine ecstasy, was discovered and developed by Vicky Wall, a chiropodist and pharmacist, through prayer and meditation. The brilliant colours and subtle fragrances are a real feast for the senses, both inner and outer. For sleep and dreams, Balance Oil no. 33, 'Dolphin', or 'Peace with a Purpose', is one of the best. It is a combination of Royal Blue and Turquoise. Apply a little with the fingertips around the jaw and hairline. Oil no. 35, 'Kindness', is Pink and Violet in colour, and especially helpful for insomnia caused by emotional problems. Apply with the fingertips all round the body.

Having chosen any one of these methods to relax and let go, you may want to add a brief meditation before you float into a productive dream-filled sleep. Meditation is not visualization or reverie. It is a withdrawal of the physical senses into a state of inner peace, stillness and silence. If prayer can be described as talking to God, or the Source of Life, meditation is listening – not only to God but to our own souls, our own true or God-selves. Meditation nourishes the spirit in the same way that the air that we breathe and the food that we eat energize the body. It is a tool for growth, change, healing and inspiration and, if practised regularly, enables us to live our lives free of fear and full of love for ourselves and others.

A simple way to begin is to make yourself comfortable, close your eyes, take a few deep breaths and silently affirm: 'I am in communion with the essence of my being.' This has a similar effect on the mind and body as if you had said: 'Be still and know that I am God.' Remain silent for at least a minute and then open your eyes or go to sleep. You can do this in the morning or at night and as you practise you may find the one minute increases to five or ten without effort.

There are hundreds of different ways to meditate, the main point to remember is that meditation is not difficult. The key is to take your mind away from the thoughts of the day and into an inner space where you let what happens happen rather than *make* it happen. Further on in the book I will give other

suggestions for meditation. Meanwhile, although visualization and reverie are not meditation, they can certainly prepare you for it and lead you into a meditative space. For example, you may prefer to imagine yourself floating away on fluffy white clouds or drifting down a river in a cushion-filled boat whose motion gently rocks you to sleep. You may have a favourite garden, meadow or mountain that you can picture yourself in or on, your face warmed by the sun, your hair slightly blown by the breeze ... You may want to wander amongst trees until you find your own personal angel of sleep. Let your imagination play and have fun. Remember that it is through fantasy and imagination that we have the power to make visible the invisible, and when we take imaginary journeys before sleep we stimulate the dreaming brain's creativity.

DIFFERENT KINDS OF DREAMS

'But I was well
Upon my way to sleep before it fell
And I could tell
What form my dreaming was about to take.'

ROBERT FROST

Dreams are powerful and accurate tools for self-discovery, healing, inspiration and problem-solving. They expand our awareness, always tell the truth and, because they interface with a wisdom and knowledge not easily available to our waking selves, present us with X-ray like pictures of what we truly think, feel and do. In Jung's words, 'The dream is a spontaneous self-portrait, in symbolic form, of the actual situation in the unconscious.'

Dream images convey to the dreamer vital information unknown to his waking consciousness. They bridge past, present and future, intellect and imagination, masculine and feminine, action and feeling, talking and listening.

When we drive a car down the street, despite rear and side view mirrors, we have a limited vision of the road and traffic around us. If we were to cover the same route in a helicopter our vision would expand to include roads ahead, behind and around us. We would see roadblocks, accidents and possible short-cuts. From this higher or wider perspective we could make decisions on how best to reach our destination and eliminate possible problems. Dreams give us the opportunity to take this 'helicopter' view of life.

While dreams can, and do, mirror the events of the day, and dream intelligence is several steps ahead of waking intelligence, dreams also express messages that come from the part of our dreaming mind that views life multidimensionally. This means that the wisdom communicated (from the unconscious to the conscious mind) is presented to us through a variety of different types of dream which can be interpreted in many ways.

RECURRING

In my experience a recurring dream is one of the most important. It is like a message from the inner to the outer self which tries to shake us awake to a problem or feeling we may have ignored, been unaware of or refused to deal with. The very fact that a dream re-occurs suggests a refusal to listen on the part of the dreamer, so repetitive dreams often shock, frighten or humour us in such a way that we are forced to pay attention. A recurring dream will (like all dreams) point out unconscious frustration, resentment or that something is wrong in our lives, but with an extra kick which, similar to a nightmare, releases a lot of repressed emotional energy.

A true recurring dream is one which is exactly the same each time and may repeat itself over a period of years – even from childhood to old age. It also suggests that the dreamer is stuck in some aspect of life and in order to move forward must both recognize and resolve the problems that hold them back.

NIGHTMARES

These are described by the Chinese as dreams of 'terror and dread'. They can jolt us awake, screaming with fright or revulsion, while sweat pours down our faces and our hearts pump with extra force as we try to escape the threat pictured in the dream scenario. According to Gayle Delaney, a renowned American dream expert, nightmares are 'dreams that develop a plot and fill you with so much anxiety or anger that you wake up from them'. She separates nightmares from night terrors by describing the latter as characterized by 'cataclysmic panic' accompanied by blood-curdling screams and disorientation on awakening. On the other hand, dramatic dreams that may frighten us but do not jolt us awake are referred to by most dream therapists as simply 'bad dreams'.

Nightmares usually involve feelings of helplessness and a sense of being out of control or at the mercy of external events and/or people. Dream research shows that children suffer more frequently from nightmares than adults, especially between the ages of three to six, and adult nightmares are often based on childhood feelings of powerlessness.

In-depth studies on the nightmare sufferer (carried out in the Shattock Hospital, Boston, USA) reveal that people with a creative bent, such as artists, musicians, writers or poets, tend to have more nightmares than manual workers or office personnel. Many of the research subjects were also found to have had difficulties in adolescence and to have rebelled against parental control by using drugs and alcohol or by running away. They were described as having 'thin boundaries' between their inner wishes and fears and the external events of their lives.

A study of pregnant women's dreams show that they reflect more anxiety and fear than dreams of other groups. (This may be because in the West, pregnancy and labour are virtually classified as illnesses rather than natural and happy processes.) Strangely, research also discovered that the more nightmares a woman had, the shorter her time in labour. Another study showed that it was not so much the quantity of nightmares, but rather their content that determined an easy labour or otherwise. The American psychologist Patricia Garfield's 1986 doctoral study of pregnant women's dreams revealed that the more assertive a woman is in a nightmare, the greater the likelihood of shorter labour.

Obviously, all of us, at some time or another have had or will have a nightmare. Rather like a recurring dream, a nightmare is a call for help, healing and attention from the inner to the outer self. If we can recognize and deal with the underlying stress or problem we can also transform both ourselves and our lives. In fact to ignore a nightmare is similar to ignoring a flashing light on the road or on the dashboard of a car. It suggests we must stop, look, listen and take some kind of action.

HEALING DREAMS

Healing dreams, which may come spontaneously or through invocation, include those that warn us of impending ill-health, crisis or accident, diagnostic dreams which clue us into the particular cause of illness as well as those dreams which do in fact heal us.

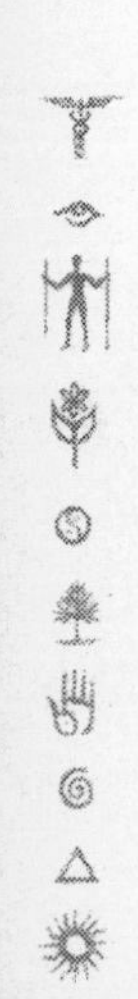

PRODOMIC DREAMS

A dream that warns us of possible ill-health is called a Prodomic dream. These often take the form of cars that run out of fuel or whose brakes fail. Buildings, machinery, clothing and vehicles are frequently used to symbolize the dreamer's body. Before we break a leg or undergo surgery we may dream of a torn piece of clothing, a collapsed building, a familiar and often used piece of equipment refusing to function, or a storm on the horizon, amongst other things.

A young girl dreamed that in 12 months she would have cancer in her right leg. She began to draw one-legged teddy bears and 12 months later her right leg was amputated.

Dreams that predict the onset of a disease or heart attack often have a nightmare quality of war, earthquake, fire or famine, or show the dreamer wounded in the part of the body that later reveals itself as malfunctioning. Months before a stomach operation I saw myself in a dream remove my dress and drop it in front of a woman who sat behind a large sewing-machine. Three or four men in white coats picked it up and began to cut into it before sewing it up again. At the time I had no conscious awareness of impending stomach problems. I have also had pneumonia a number of times and before one of the worst attacks I dreamed someone threw an axe at my chest and my lungs filled with blood.

Another health warning dream can be that of a policeman pointing out defective lights, flat tyres or a faulty exhaust on one's car. A friend who tends to party a little too much knows that when she dreams of an old, wise woman admonishing her to slow down she will usually end up in bed a few days later.

Prodomic dreams can also depict a friend or colleague with symptoms that apply to oneself. An example of this is Freud's dream of Irma, one of his patients, in which he saw in her all the symptoms of the throat cancer from which he later suffered.

But prodomic dreams do give us the chance to act before we become ill. Patricia Garfield suggests we should record our dreams and review them from time to time to check for health warnings. We should look at our dreams when we feel exceptionally healthy as well as those preceding and during illness. Garfield says, 'One important clue to your health in dreams is contained in the rate of activity in your dream images. When

your metabolism changes from normal to too fast or too slow, your dream figures grow correspondingly over-active or inactive.'

DIAGNOSTIC DREAMS

These dreams reveal the cause of physical problems, often when modern medical science has failed to do so. A good example is the case described by Bernie Segal, the American physician and surgeon who is well known for his work with cancer patients. The dreamer was a nurse who had been sick for weeks without anyone being able to discover what was wrong with her. She finally dreamed of a shellfish that opened, revealing a worm that stood up inside it. An old woman pointed at the worm and said, 'That's what is wrong with you.' When the nurse awoke she was sure she had hepatitis A – a liver infection caused by eating shellfish from contaminated water. Her dream used the worm as a metaphor for the virus. Subsequent tests confirmed the diagnosis.

Bernie Segal believes that all doctors should examine the images presented by the unconscious in their patients' dreams. He says this goes beyond what a patient may say on the surface and reveals what is really going on inside their minds as well as their bodies.

One of the most famous of all dream diagnosticians was Galen, a physician who lived AD 129–199. Galen became a doctor after his father had a dream in which Asklepios, the Greek god of healing, commanded him to have his son trained as a physician. At one time Galen became seriously ill and went to one of the healing temples dedicated to Asklepios and asked for dreams to show him what was wrong and how to cure himself. His dreams showed him he had a mass of infected fluid under the diaphragm and over the liver and that he should open an artery in his hand between his thumb and forefinger and let it bleed until it stopped. He did this and was cured. Galen used dreams as a diagnostic tool throughout his life and often treated his patients with remedies based on them.

In both Russia and America, many hospitals are now investigating their patients' dreams to see if it is possible to correlate certain dreams with specific illness and disease. One Russian psychiatrist, Vasili Kasatkin, has reportedly saved hundreds of lives by using his patients' dreams to diagnose ill-health long before it either manifested in the body or could be picked up by orthodox tests. Kasatkin says that different illnesses follow clearly defined dream patterns which could be used as an early warning system for both patients and doctors.

HEALING DREAMS

A truly healing dream is one when we go to sleep sick and, through the dream process, wake up healed. Inscriptions giving thanks to Asklepios in ancient healing sites such as Epidaurus in Greece testify that this type of miraculous healing has occurred since the earliest recorded history. One of the most impressive cases was that of a paralysed girl who, unable to go to the temple and ask for healing herself, sent a friend to do so on her behalf. That night, in a dream, Asklepios appeared to her and said, 'Why aren't you in the temple?' When she replied, 'I cannot move,' Asklepios said, 'Well then, I will heal you here.' In the morning when the girl awoke she found she could walk.

More recently, an alcoholic friend of mine, Max, dreamt that Muktananda, an Indian guru who died in 1982, tapped him on the head with a peacock feather. He awoke cured of his addiction to vodka and never had any desire to drink alcohol again. Max had never heard of Muktananda until his name appeared in the dream.

A similar case was that of Alison, who had throat cancer and who dreamed that flames were burning her throat. Ali Baba then appeared with his magic lamp and told her that if she rubbed it with her hands, ash would appear which she must then use to douse the flames. Confused by her dream, Alison shared it with a friend who told her about Sai Baba, the Indian holy man who is considered to be a reincarnated god by many of his followers. Sai Baba manifests ash from his hands, which thousands of people, who use it world-wide, believe to have an almost magical effect on their lives and their health. Alison's friend was, by strange (or pre-planned, from a super-conscious level) synchronicity, about to visit Sai Baba in India for the third time. Alison accompanied her, received into her own hands some of Sai Baba's ash and massaged it over a period of days into her neck. She returned home cured. The dream itself did not heal her but put into her hands the means of a cure.

Healing dreams will sometimes tell us exactly what to do, such as Galen's dream in which he was told to open an artery. Others may initially be more concerned with healing our psyche rather than our body. Illness, accident, rape or any kind of violence that causes physical injury induce feelings of helplessness and vulnerability. At these times any dream that encourages us to take action and/or control suggests that we have the power to overcome the situation. Even if we do not remember the entire dream scenario, we may wake up full of strength and determination, no longer victims of our problems but willing to take responsibility for them.

Mary, in her 70s, entered a London hospital to have a heart and lung transplant. The night before the operation, apprehensive and depressed, she wished she had refused to undergo such major surgery because at her age the prognosis for survival was not good. Mary's attitude to her body was that it belonged to the doctors and not to her, so she must let them do what they liked with it. That night she dreamed a nurse asked her how she was feeling. 'Terrible,' Mary replied. 'I'm sure I'm going to die and rather than die in a hospital bed I would prefer to be at home with my husband and dogs.' The nurse reminded Mary that she was responsible for herself and her body and must do what was best for her. She offered to get Mary a taxi so she could return home. Mary was shocked and said, 'But I must not upset the doctors.' The nurse showed Mary a clipboard on which was a list of all the health crises in Mary's life. In a stern voice she said, 'Each time, if you had taken better care of your body, these traumas would have been less severe.'

Mary awoke, shocked at the truth of what the dream nurse had said. At dawn she called for the hospital night nurse and said she had decided she would be happier and more comfortable spending her last days at home, so please would the nurse telephone for a taxi. The nurse told Mary she could not take responsibility for this as Mary was too ill to leave. Buoyed up by her dream, Mary insisted the nurse call a taxi and quietly added, 'My body, health and happiness are all my responsibility and no one else's.' She spent the last six months of her life at home, in her garden, surrounded by everyone and everything she loved.

Mary's dream did not heal her body but it did change her attitude to it and enabled her to enjoy the time she had left instead of suffering the wounds and subsequent discomfort of surgery.

One of my own healing dreams told me to stop feeling so sorry for myself and study indigenous peoples' methods of healing. As a result I became involved with crystals, meditation, visualization, affirmation, therapeutic touch, the power of thought and a number of other disciplines, which changed my life as well as healed my body. Another healing dream, one that came at a time of great crisis in my life, forced me to confront despair, rage, pain and fear in such a way that I learned the only way to overcome a black time in one's life is to merge with the blackness and thereby transform it, rather than resist it. This same dream showed me that no matter what calamity erupts in our lives, if we give in to it, it has power over us. When we fight back, however, we rob the problem of its power. The energy of this dream got me out of bed and on my feet, at three in the morning, after months of physical, mental and emotional paralysis.

During convalescence, after illness, accident or surgery, healing dreams may initially replay the trauma, but later tend to comfort and soothe. The dreamer may both see and sense warm hands stroking or massaging the body; animals cavorting in fields or meadows lush with green grass and wild flowers; gardens, plants, trees, flowers, buds opening; snakes that uncoil or shed a skin; seas that change from choppy to crystal clear and calm; cloudy skies that become blue or filled with twinkling stars; the sun or sunlight pouring through a window or bathing the body in golden yellow light. Amongst other dreams which depict recovery are those in which the dreamer clears or tidies a house, a room, a chest of drawers or kitchen cupboards; weeds a garden, scatters seeds or plants flowers; gives birth to a baby or finds a young child that needs love and care; chooses new clothes or uninhibitedly throws off old ones. Sensual or sexual feelings in convalescent dreams also symbolize recovery and ultimate return to health.

We can even invoke healing dreams to speed recovery during illness (see pages 39–42).

PROPHETIC, PRECOGNITIVE AND TELEPATHIC DREAMS

While psychiatrists and psychologists in the West are now trying to get us to reconnect with our dreams, indigenous people have never been cut off from theirs. Prophetic and telepathic dreams which can guide, warn and inform are cultivated by most tribes and used as a means of survival in the same way that we might switch on the radio or television to get a weather or traffic report before we set off on a journey, or a political or financial forecast before we buy or sell shares or houses.

Historically, 'dreams of divination' have been crucial to the lives of many people, prominent and otherwise, predicting success in battle for people as diverse as Genghis Khan, Oliver Cromwell, Napoleon, Constantine and Hitler. Jung and many others had terrifying, precognitive dreams about the Second World War.

Although prophetic, precognitive, clairvoyant and telepathic dreams are similar, prophetic dreams are usually concerned with future, more impersonal, wider, community or even global issues. Precognitive dreams are usually more personal and give us a waking, intuitive hunch that suggests we do not catch the train, plane or bus that subsequently crashes, or that we keep our children at home from school for the day – as one Dunfermline mother did in response to a dream on the day of the dreadful Dunblane massacre.

A predictive or clairvoyant dream is one which provides us with information about events of which we have no conscious knowledge. It is similar to a psychic reading and can only be truly assessed if the events prophesied subsequently take place.

Telepathic or clairvoyant dreams tend to put us in touch with and show us people and events not in our immediate environment. These vary between personal and impersonal – telepathic dreams may concern a member of the family in trouble or present a clairvoyant image of a complete stranger.

For example, John, wheelchair bound, read in a newspaper that a young local girl had disappeared on her way home from school. That night he dreamed the exact details of what had

happened and where she was. In the morning he called the police and, despite their scepticism, they searched for an area that matched his description. To their (and even John's) amazement, they found the girl dirty, hungry and exhausted, but alive, exactly as John's dream depicted.

Another example is that of Joelene, who had to leave her 15-year-old son Martin with her divorced husband while she worked in America for six months. After four weeks, she dreamed she met Martin on the street, looking miserable, with his shoulders loaded with bricks. Awake, she telephoned him and discovered he was desperate because of the weight of responsibility loaded on him by his father. Accordingly, she made different arrangements that enabled Martin to join her in America. Subsequently everyone was happy.

Prophetic or precognitive dreams are quite common, but most of us either pay no attention or dismiss them as fantasy. Usually they come with a gut feeling that impels us to act on what the dream said. In my own experience these dreams and my subsequent use of them have, on two or three occasions, saved my life.

DREAMS OF COMPENSATION

In the words of Jung, 'The general function of dreams is to restore our psychological balance by producing dream material that re-establishes, in a subtle way, the total psychic equilibrium.' Compensatory dreams do exactly that. They bring emotional balance by encouraging us to express facets of our personality we are either unable or unwilling to express while awake. In other words, these dreams show us an opposite side of ourselves, which can bring us sharply down to earth if we feel superior to, or critical of, others and push us to stand up for ourselves if we lack self-love and acceptance.

In his book, *Man and his Symbols* Jung describes the recurring dream of an extremely difficult and argumentative woman. In this dream she saw herself beautifully dressed, arriving for a party. Her hostess greeted her at the door, saying, 'All the friends you know are here.' She then ushered the dreamer into a cow-filled barn. This dream helped the woman to become a little more humble.

An angry, critical and extremely arrogant man I know dreamed he was put in stocks in the middle of Leicester Square by the very people he mocked and criticized. They removed his trousers and threw rotten fruit and vegetables at him until he begged for release. Two policemen appeared and said, 'Sir, we cannot release you until you promise to mend your ways.' The man promised and awoke. The impact of the dream helped him, too, to become more humane and less judgemental.

On the other hand, Jack, brought up in an orphanage and vulnerable and a little afraid of life, had recurring dreams in which he saw himself as a John Wayne-type cowboy shooting at his boss. The shots he fired never actually hit his boss's body, but knocked his hat off or pinned his jacket to a wall. In waking life, Jack's boss was a mean bully and no matter how hard Jack worked, he was never satisfied. Because Jack needed the job and was afraid of his boss, he never answered back. His dreams gave him the opportunity to express a part of himself impossible while awake and gradually encouraged him to fight back. As he did so, his bullying boss, like most bullies, began to back down and treat Jack with respect.

Another type of compensatory dream is the one that lets us explore an unlived part that has been denied expression because of the life choices we've made. For example, Madeleine trained as a ballet dancer but, at the height of her career, fell in love, married and went on to have four children. Whenever she

saw newspaper articles that described her old ballet company's success, she felt a pang of regret for the choice she'd made – especially when engulfed by nappies, bottles and her young children's endless demands. Then Madeleine began to dream that she was still a dancer. She saw herself touring the world, successful, fêted and applauded wherever she went. She experienced the elation when bouquets of roses were thrown at her feet after every performance. For almost a year, Madeleine's dreams allowed her to experience everything she felt she'd missed out on by getting married. The dreams fulfilled her to such an extent that she no longer compared 'the life that might have been' to the one she had.

A similar dream was the one of Liam, an Irish priest, who, at 40, began to think longingly of children and family. He wondered if he should leave the ministry and prayed long and hard for an answer to his spiritual dilemma. Dreams began to unfold in which he saw himself as a Provençal peasant farmer, with a fat little Italian wife. Together they ploughed the fields, argued volubly, made love frequently and raised a large and happy family. For Liam, these dreams allowed him to experience a richly emotional night life which compensated for his disciplined, celibate waking life.

SHADOW DREAMS

The Shadow is the term used to describe aspects of ourselves that, consciously or unconsciously, we find unacceptable. We see our Shadow mirrored back to us in everyone who repulses, irritates or upsets us, subconsciously recognizing in them the exact habits, mannerisms and behaviour we dislike in ourselves. In fact we project these attributes onto them – which may lead to our being surrounded by angry, impatient or helpless people who simply reflect what is denied in us.

The more we repress our 'nasty' or Shadow side, the more power and energy we feed into it. This repression can later turn into illness, depression, accident-proneness or outlandish behaviour completely at odds with what was normal before.

In dreams the Shadow may often appear as dark, evil, ugly and frightening. To become whole (perfectly whole, that is, not wholly perfect), we must befriend our Shadow, transform it and lift it to another level. Once we accept this hidden or dark side of ourselves – which may come through a struggle to overcome an addictive pattern of behaviour – we will always find unexpected gifts that transform our lives.

During a particularly traumatic phase of my life, when day after day I felt as if I were suffocating in a thick black fog, I dreamed I was dragging my body inch by inch up a mountain made of huge, rough steps. Each step was as tall as my body. I could reach the next one only by standing on tiptoe and straining to get my fingertips over the edge. By the time I reached the top my body was scratched raw and bleeding. Confronting me was a thick, monstrous mass of black, evil-looking slime. I knew that it symbolized the sum total of all the terrible things that had happened in my life combined with all my fears of what might happen.

Revulsed I turned to go back down the mountain but was too afraid of the height to do so. Transfixed with fear I turned to face the blackness, and almost involuntarily my fist smashed into and merged with it. Immediately the dark slime exploded into thousands of glittering, crystal rainbows that cascaded around me, filling the air with light and colour. The effect was so electrifying that it woke me up. It was 3am but I leapt out of bed bursting with energy and eager to get on with my life.

My dream forced me (compelled me?) to recognize that as long as I resisted the dark, it grew. When I confronted and merged with it, I could transform it – and so it is for all of us.

BIG AND LITTLE DREAMS

For me, a little dream offers a running commentary on personal issues, such as family, work or health. A big dream reflects a wider perspective – such as Jung's precognitive dreams of the Second World War – and often leads to a radical change of belief and personality.

SEXUAL DREAMS

Sexuality in dreams, often to the point of orgasm, frequently occurs as the result of lucid dreams, i.e. becoming aware of dreaming in the dream. Whether lucid or otherwise, sexual dreams can shock, frighten, tantalize or embarrass us. They encompass the complete range of sexual experience, from straightforward joy of sex to masturbation, sex in unusual positions, sex in extraordinary and often public places, sex with familiar or famous people, sex interrupted by parents and/or others, heterosexual sex, homosexual sex and even sex-change as well as incest, rape and other forms of sexual violation.

Instead of feeling guilty or embarrassed by such dreams, we should joyfully accept them – unless of course they are unpleasant, in which case we must delve into the underlying reasons for this.

Dream research shows that both men and women who have frequent sexually explicit dreams which arouse fear or unhappiness tend to repress or ignore problems in waking life. These are not necessarily just sexual problems. Men and women whose sexual dreams are joyful, humorous and satisfying, on the other hand, tend to face and overcome their problems far more easily. It also appears that people who openly discuss sexual dreams are far more creative than those who are too shy or embarrassed to do so.

Many therapists today encourage sexually inhibited or frigid patients to incubate or ask for sexual dreams as part of their treatment. They find that not only does a dream tell far more about a person's attitude to self, sex and sexual relationships than discussion, but it also, by allowing the dreamer to explore specific sexual activities they may never have tried before, improves their waking sex life.

People who appear in our dreams, whether these are sexual or otherwise, should always be interpreted as aspects of ourselves first, despite what secondary or even multi-level meaning they might also have. This means that no matter if we dream of making love to the milkman, the boss, a member of the Royal Family, Brigitte Bardot or our next-door neighbour, our dream mind is pushing us to recognize and merge with the qualities in us that are symbolized by this other personality. So, while sexual dreams *can* loosen our attitude to sexuality, when they involve other people, whether known or unknown, they also symbolize union with different parts of ourselves. Even if we dream of making love with someone of our own sex, we are not merely blatantly or latently homosexual, but are reinforcing our own masculine and feminine energy and attributes, as well as the qualities of the man or woman in the dream. If a sexual dream partner repulses us, we must also look at why, and what in ourselves is similarly repulsive.

Not all sexual dreams are sexually explicit – some use metaphors and symbols to guide and instruct. Dr Gayle Delaney, who runs the Delaney and Flowers Dream Center in San Francisco, describes a client's dream in which, during a piano lesson, his teacher instructed him not to storm the keys but to treat the piano as a sensitive instrument which would then produce beautiful music. The dreamer later recognized his attitude to sex was more like that of a storm-trooper than a musician.

Often dreams in which we find ourselves in bed with one or more people denote current or future work together, while a chaste kiss on the lips or cheek is a symbol of brotherly love and spiritual kinship.

Unfortunately, in the West, many religions teach us that sex is either sinful or solely for procreation. So we grow up with no understanding of the connection between sexuality, spirituality and creativity. I read recently that sexual energy is close to spiritual energy and personally, I do not believe there is a difference. It is simply the undifferentiated energy of the universe which we use to talk, walk, draw, sing, paint, write, knit and/or dig a garden, as well as make love. It is the energy of creation which we channel into hundreds of different pursuits every single day. Therefore to encourage and enjoy sexual expression in our dreams will stimulate more spontaneity and creativity in our waking lives.

As Jung said of Freud, 'He wanted to teach – or so at least it seemed to me – that regarded from within, sexuality included spirituality and had an intrinsic meaning.'

We can bring about, or incubate, sexual dreams by simply writing down, before sleep, what we would like to experience in the dream. If it is a request for a dream to solve a sexual problem, it helps to write a few notes about the problem and your attitude to it first. Then simply write, in your own words: 'I want a dream that clarifies the source of my problem and how I may overcome it; or, if, say, you feel your sexual problem is your own inadequacy, 'I am embarrassed about my body being too fat, thin, tall, small, etc., so give me a dream that will improve my self-image.'

You can also use this type of incubation to ask for a dream lover if you are resistant to the idea of or do not currently have a waking-life lover. If you do this, make a few pre-sleep notes about the kind of lover you'd like to meet in your dreams –

humorous, kind, passionate, older, younger, tall, short, dark or blond, handsome, beautiful, plain, ugly or somewhere in between, whatever appeals to you.

Many of my partnerless friends have done this in disbelief and jest, only to find they had such a good time in their dreams (usually following the pattern of a normal courtship and not automatically involving sexuality) that they stopped actively searching for a waking-life partner. Then, as soon as they relaxed and enjoyed the various men in their lives as human beings, rather than as prospective marriage partners, the man of their dreams appeared on the scene.

ARCHETYPES IN DREAMS

Jung introduced us to the idea of the collective unconscious, the complex, archetypes, animus and anima, introvert and extravert, the persona, the Shadow, synchronicity and the process of individuation. For him, the collective unconscious contained the wisdom of the ages and was a level of mind that was impersonal, transpersonal, the source of all. It evolved consciously and was the place where all men are one. Laurens van der Post, a friend of Jung's, described it as 'an area in which the whole of life participates, as it were, mystically'.

Arising out of the collective unconscious are primordial, universal images that symbolize certain character traits, behaviour and energy patterns that Jung called 'archetypes'. An archetype is an innate, spontaneously recurring pattern within the collective psyche of all mankind. Jung found the same symbols occurred as much with primitive people, cut off from civilization, as with those well versed in myths, art and religion. People with no religious background dreamed of angels and devils, while others saw Roman slaves, Aztec princesses, witches, magicians or wise men.

In the past, archetypal figures popped up in our dreams in the shape of gods, goddesses, heroes, heroines, the wise old man or woman, the hermit, warrior queen, trickster, witch mother or innocent child, amongst many others. Today's archetypes are more likely to appear in the form of currently popular movie or television stars, politicians, public figures, actors, actresses and even the imaginary heroes and heroines from books. So, well known personalities such as Queen Elizabeth II, the Queen Mother, Princess Diana, Mother Teresa, Eva Peron, Nelson Mandela, Churchill, President Kennedy, Madonna and Marilyn Monroe can all appear as archetypes in our dreams.

Animals are also used by our dreaming selves as archetypal symbols for particular instincts, although some have other archetypal meanings – the dove, for example, is considered to be an archetypal manifestation of the Holy Spirit.

Archetypes function in our psyches in much the same way as our instincts function in our bodies: they represent inner conflicts, strengths and weaknesses, patterns of energy which, if we can understand their symbology, give us the capacity to move through life's challenges more easily. In fact the more unaware we are of these archetypal energies, the more power they have to rule our lives.

Myths, legends, fairy tales, plays, films, paintings, music, historical characters and events, even fictional characters and events – anything which evokes feeling, thought, intuition and sensation – can tap us into archetypal memories, release blocked energy and then inspire creative action in our daily lives. Ancient stories about gods and goddesses, King Arthur and the Knights of the Round Table, Parsifal's search for the Grail, Shakespeare's plays – all describe archetypal situations which, when we interpret their real meaning, we can use to better understand our own lives today.

For example, in the Greek myth of Psyche and Aphrodite, Psyche is set four 'do or die' tasks, which initially overwhelm her. The first is to sort the seeds of the world overnight, which means we must sort out our priorities if we want to find fulfilment and happiness in our lives. The second is to gather wool from the Golden Fleece, who are wild rams with a tendency to gore people to death. This means we must use enough male energy to do what we want to do but not so much that we become aggressive bullies. (Male energy is active and outwardly expressive; it is *doing*. Female energy is passive, inward looking, sensing, feeling; *being*, rather than doing.) The third task is to fill a crystal goblet with water from the River Styx, which runs in a raging torrent from high mountains into the Underworld. This means that we must have a crystal-clear idea of what we want to achieve in life before we set out to accomplish it. We can fill as many goblets as we want, but we need to focus on one project at a time to ensure total success. The fourth task requires Psyche to descend into the Underworld to get a jar of Queen Persephone's beauty cream for Aphrodite. This means we must be willing to descend into the depths of ourselves to find our own hidden beauty and value.

However, as important as the task itself is the advice Psyche is given for her journey. She has two coins to pay a ferryman to take her to the Underworld and back and is told to go straight there and to give *no* help to anyone on the way. Various people beg for help or money and finally Psyche's refusal to help allows a man to drown while she watches. This means we have exactly what we need – energy, ability and knowledge (the two coins) – to accomplish what we came to Earth for. If we do not learn to say no, in love, we will squander our time and energy and never fulfil what we came here to do. To watch the man drown sounds very cruel but it is a test of love to let someone drown in the result of their own experience rather than help them out of it. I refer here to drug addicts, alcoholics, criminals, etc., who use our help just to stay where they are. If they are allowed to 'drown', they hit rock bottom and so can only come up. I am not suggesting we never help anyone, but if we help others to the extent that we have nothing left for ourselves, we are misusing our power.

The story of Psyche and Aphrodite is about the evolution of consciousness and confidence in a woman, whereas the medieval legend of Parsifal, the Holy Grail and the Fisher King is about the masculine evolution of consciousness. Both stories are well worth reading because they inspire archetypal dream dramas as well as stir up unconscious and subconscious memories.

Another way to stimulate archetypal dreams is to study the Tarot. Tarot cards symbolize the instinctual forces embedded in the psyche. They also depict some of the major themes and experiences we will have on our journey through life. The Major Arcana show archetypal figures that can inform and inspire us, while the Minor Arcana give an understanding of some of the people and challenges we are likely to meet on our way.

There are many excellent books on the Tarot but I suggest that the best way to begin is to study each card in turn and note any reactions, ideas, memories and associations that come to mind. Trust your first impressions and do not censor them. Ask yourself which card or cards appear to be the most applicable to your life today and ask for a dream to expand on this. Copy or trace the cards in a meditative way, then colour them in. This stimulates imagination and awareness. As you sum up what the cards mean to you, look around at the people in your life and see if a particular personality matches a card. Ask for dreams to explain why this person or situation is in your life today – whether good or bad – and then apply the information or understanding to your life.

If you dream of an archetypal figure from the past or the present, note any words, thoughts and feelings you associate with that personality. If the image is frightening, mentally surround it with light and ask the child in it to appear or mentally shrink it to a smaller, less powerful size. Ask yourself questions such as 'What part of me, or what qualities in me, does X represent?' 'What does X's presence in my dream tell me?' 'What action in my waking life does X encourage me to take?' 'Who does X remind me of?' 'How can X heal or help me?'

With practice, this type of exercise can reveal all sorts of hidden fears and blocks caused by our own unconscious beliefs as well as give an insight into the toolbox of strengths, talents and abilities each of us was born with.

DREAM JOURNEYS

> The real voyage of discovery consists not in seeing new landscapes but in having new eyes.
>
> MARCEL PROUST

While all dreams interface with a source of wisdom and knowledge far beyond our waking consciousness, the following dreams are virtually supernatural, or paranormal, and stimulate a greater awareness of invisible worlds.

DREAMS OF ASTRAL TRAVEL

Whether we believe it or not, or are aware of it or not, we all travel astrally during sleep. The astral or dream body is the etheric counterpart to the physical.

It is roughly the same size and shape as the earthly body, and can detach from it and move about. The astral body features in many spiritual doctrines, especially those from the East. For most primitive people the astral travels during sleep are *real* experiences undertaken by the soul. It is therefore considered dangerous to wake a sleeping person suddenly, in case the astral body is too far away from the physical to enter it at once.

The astral body is connected to the physical by what is known as the silver cord, a long filmy cord that is broken at death. When we sleep and dream, the astral body lifts out of the physical and explores other dimensions, but remains connected by the silver cord. If the astral body gets too involved in its exploration of other realms, or too far away, the physical body automatically jerks it back and tightens the connecting cord with such a jolt that we can awake with a sense of falling, shock and nausea. (This is quite different from a dream of falling.)

Although sometimes described as the spiritual body, the astral body is neither the soul nor spirit of man but rather a vehicle for the soul – a little like the bulb around a light filament. It has one level ruled by emotion and desire and another, altruistic level which is governed by care and concern for others.

The ancient Egyptians believed that the astral body, or Ka, was the immortal, spiritual double of a man. The hieroglyph for it was a star. Paracelsus, the alchemist, doctor, chemist and philosopher, described the astral body as a star body which lives beside the physical and is its mirror image.

Hereward Carrington and Sylvan Muldoon, authors of *The Projection of the Astral Body*, define the astral body as the ethereal counterpart of the physical, composed of a semi-fluidic or subtle form of matter usually invisible to the human eye. Some psychics can see it, however, and describe it as an etheric mist or vapour not perceptible to the touch, or as a luminous radiance that surrounds and interpenetrates the body. When seen around the body it is usually described as the aura, although many clairvoyants say the aura is one of three shells that enclose the soul and mind and although it may interpenetrate the astral body it is different from it.

The astral body of a dying person can often be seen hovering beside or above the physical, or even hundreds of miles away, if there is a strong desire to see someone before death. There are many war-time stories of soldiers who suddenly appeared to their families a few hours before an official notice of death was

received. A 90-year-old friend remembers her doctor father appearing to her while she sat at a window awaiting his return home at the end of the day. She rose to greet him and her hand went through his body. He then gradually faded away. A few minutes later a messenger arrived to say he had died in an accident on the way home. Having seen her father enabled my friend to cope more easily with the pain and the shock of his loss.

Spontaneous or involuntary ejections from the physical into the astral body can be caused by sudden crisis, shock, acute pain, anaesthesia, drugs, illness, chronic tiredness, stress, accident and extreme fear. When Ernest Hemingway was 19 and serving as a soldier in Italy, he was standing in a trench when an Austrian mortar shell loaded with scrap metal landed close by. Thinking he was dead, he said, 'I felt my soul or something coming right out of my body, like you'd pull a silk handkerchief out of a pocket by one corner. It flew around and then came back and went in again and I wasn't dead any more.' Hemingway later used the incident in his book *Farewell to Arms*.

While most of us astral travel unconsciously during sleep, spiritual teachers and yogis such as Paramhansa Yogananda and Madame Blavatsky, founder of the Theosophical Society, used astral projection regularly to communicate with fellow teachers, adepts and great masters. Yogananda's book *Autobiography of a Yogi* contains many stories about the projection of the astral body to distant places, and other occult books such as *the Masters of the Far East* by Baird T. Spalding describe how discarnate masters use their astral bodies to convene in groups on mountain tops or arid, desert land.

We can learn to consciously free the astral body from the physical by following spiritual disciplines such as yoga and meditation. We can also practise projecting our consciousness into a tree, a rock, a flower, a friend's house or even another country. The key is to visualize or imagine the sensation of being inside a tree etc., while your body remains on the bed or the chair.

Another simple exercise which can help trigger astral travel is to imagine the etheric or invisible body lifting out of the physical and hovering above it. Do this with your eyes closed. After a few minutes mentally move the etheric body left and then right. Notice any different sensations and then focus on a place you love to visit or would like to go to. In your imagination explore every facet of the place. If necessary, get photos from travel magazines or travel agents and study them to get as full a picture in your mind as possible beforehand. Also remember your body needs to be fully relaxed. Any of the exercises described in the chapter on sleep preparation can be used for this. It is usually when we are in the slightly hazy stage in between waking and sleeping that we can lift out of the body. I recommend saying a brief prayer or a few words to invoke protection before you do this. To learn to lucid dream at will is another good way to prepare for astral travel.

You can also release yourself from the physical body more easily through the use of stones. Black star provides protection and keeps you connected to the Earth while you astral travel. It also helps to ground you when you return. Celestite calms and relaxes mind and body, assists in contacting angelic guardians and guides, and protects while astral travelling. Moldavite, supposedly the result of a meteorite falling to Earth, facilitates astral travel and helps develop spiritual insight. Amazarite also makes astral travel easier and aligns the physical and astral bodies on return.

Always make sure you ground yourself properly after your journeys, even if they are imaginary, rather than truly astral. You can do this by breathing deeply, yawning, stretching, pressing your feet firmly to the floor and your fingers into anything

solid such as the arm of a chair or a table, and humming or chanting.

Whether consciously or unconsciously practised (in sleep), astral travel prepares us for other worlds – worlds that dreams themselves introduce us to. However exciting it may sound to gad about free of the body, we need to remember we are here to enjoy and explore every facet of our physical senses while we are here on Earth – to be in the body, not out of it. Astral travel can reinforce the belief that consciousness exists in and out of the body, but we should not become addicted to its practice.

LUCID DREAMS

A lucid dream is when we become fully aware of dreaming during the dream. We can then take charge of the dream and change it at will. In a pre-lucid dream, which is quite common, we have a vague sense of dreaming but not enough awareness to take some kind of action.

Sleep clinics around the world are increasingly interested in lucid dreams and also in training dreamers to have them at will. Alan Worsley, a psychologist in a London hospital, discovered as a boy that by calling his mother's name while dreaming he could wake himself into lucidity. He says that he knows he is dreaming if he can levitate or push his hand into a table. Alan can produce, on demand, lucid dreams in which he carries out pre-arranged activities which are monitored on tape.

Lucid dreams often include a sense of flying and Alan says, 'I have lots of fun flying over landscapes, water, doing acrobats and flying backwards.' Marjorie, another 'professional' lucid-dreamer, recognizes she is dreaming when she appears to fly through the glass walls of the greenhouses in Kew Gardens.

Jeremy Taylor, a Unitarian Minister in San Francisco, says that he attempted to incubate lucid dreams by concentrating on the idea that he would fly before going to sleep. He describes a lucid dream in which he was cheerfully flying, and altering at whim the landscape around him, when he overheard a group of wise men saying in disappointed tones, 'There he goes, flying again!' In the middle of his dream he suddenly realized he was becoming distracted from his work by his focus on lucid dreaming.

Carlos Castaneda, who has recounted the sorcerer Don Juan's mysterious teachings in a series of books, learned to explore many altered states of consciousness. He describes how he was taught to induce lucid dreaming by staring at his hands for 10 minutes before sleep. In his dreams the image of his hands would then stimulate a spontaneous recognition that he was dreaming, at which point he was meant to take control. Castaneda also described the 'dreambody' and how sorcerers use it to recreate themselves in weird ways and in different realities. His books aroused world-wide interest as, for many readers, they broke barriers between the material and supernatural worlds for the first time.

However, conscious or lucid dreaming has been taught by many religions and cultures for centuries. From ancient Egyptian civilizations and so-called 'primitive' tribes to Hindu, Buddhist and Taoist religions (amongst many others), the belief that the worlds we see in our dreams are identical to the worlds we will experience after death are virtually the same.

The Tibetan Book of the Dead, for example, was specifically written to help the soul, after death, move through different stages of the Bardo world without fear. The Bardo is, in effect, the world of dreams and illusions and as we pass through it we face a multitude of self-created thought forms. Therefore, for Tibetan Buddhists, learning to remain conscious during a dream is a vital part of the spiritual preparation for death.

The Egyptians believed in a similar Bardo-like state, where the soul is judged and all the different aspects of personality

must be integrated before it moves on. Instructions on how to do this were inscribed on the walls of their tombs and wrapped up with the corpse when it was buried.

For a tribal shaman or medicine man, lucid or conscious dreaming, in which he must also take control, is vital to his work. It is in this state of altered but focused consciousness that he will commune with the spirits of his ancestors and various other mystical or supernatural beings, who will give him information, guidance and help. A shaman's training is long and arduous. He undergoes a breakdown of his physical, mental, emotional and spiritual senses in order to break through into a different level of awareness. In his dreams, a trainee shaman will face dismemberment, disembowelment, flying, song-singing, the appearance of animals, birds, fish and other mysterious and sometimes terrifying creatures who will heal and help him, if he can face them without fear. This too is similar to some of the images described in *The Tibetan Book of the Dead*.

Today, while many therapists are fascinated by lucid dreams, others fear that trying to stimulate and control what is produced by our unconscious or higher consciousness could be damaging to our waking personality. Personally, I believe that the world-wide increase of lucid dreams is symbolic of the planetary consciousness changing from a purely physical, material focus to one that is far more spiritual. Lucid dreams show we can exist in many dimensions at once and that our intelligence is not merely confined to our physical bodies. We can use this intelligence in and out of the body. Many philosophies teach that life is a dream, an illusion: 'To change your life, change your thinking.' A lucid dream, in which we take action to change what is happening in the dream, is no different. Lucid dreams expand our consciousness. This is what is needed as we move towards the year 2000.

OUT-OF-BODY EXPERIENCES

An OBE, or out-of-body experience, not a dream as such, but is very similar to astral travel. However, an OBE usually occurs as the result of a near-death experience, an accident or severe illness. The out-of-body consciousness either stays near the body and can later describe in detail everything that took place around it, or has a profound spiritual experience in which it lifts up into a place of unearthly beauty and feels illuminated with love, light and compassion – to the point where it often does not wish to return to Earth. A genuine OBE is very different from telepathy, clairvoyance or ESP (extra sensory perception), all of which enable those who have such gifts to see and know what is happening in places far removed from their physical sight. While astral travel and OBEs can both change our perspective on life, an OBE appears to be more truly spiritually transformative.

An example of this is the case of an agnostic American General who was undergoing major surgery. He was anaesthetized so heavily that during the operation his doctors feared he would never recover. The surgeon, tense from the intricacies of the operation, snapped angrily at his assistants and later swore at them when he discovered instruments he needed had not been sterilized. He ran out of the room to get his own instrument bag. When the General eventually came to, he described how, as soon as his body became comatose, he moved away from it – with, to his astonishment, full possession of his mental faculties. He went on to describe the operation, the surgeon's curses – and even the inside of the surgeon's bag. This experience opened the General's eyes to an awareness that life exists beyond the physical.

Elisabeth Kübler-Ross, the well-known psychiatrist and instigator of ground-breaking treatment for the dying, describes

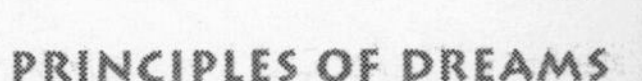

how some of her patients, even those who were blind, told her stories of what they saw and experienced out of the body during surgery or chronic illness. They were able to describe the clothing and position of the nurses in the wards or operating theatres, as well as their conversations. Elisabeth Kübler-Ross later had her own OBEs, which convinced her of life after death.

A few years ago, *Readers' Digest* magazine ran an article in which a number of near-fatal accident victims were interviewed. The accidents included falling off mountains while climbing, being stuck in rocky tunnels while pot-holing and nearly drowning during deep-sea diving, as well as being struck by lightning, falling down the stairs at home and having other 'household accidents', which included car smashes. In every case the 'victim' described ejection from the physical body instants before the accident occurred. From outside the physical body they witnessed what happened to it with curiosity rather than with fear or pain. They were later able to describe every detail of their later rescue and resuscitation.

My own first conscious OBE happened spontaneously through illness, but I later determined to leave my body at will. I spent six months, in between working and sleeping, attempting to do so without success. Frustrated, I finally decided I was wasting valuable time and energy and gave up. The very day I decided to stop, I lay down on my bed to read and suddenly found myself standing beside my bed, outside my body. I was so excited I had absolutely no control and, after whirling around the room, flew through the wall of my apartment and out onto the street about six feet (2 metres) off the ground. I zoomed into a supermarket and flew around the shelves looking at food and prices, as well as the checkout girls' faces, in order to confirm my experience later. I was totally conscious, clear and objective. Because I was in an unfamiliar part of Sydney, Australia, where I was then living, I noted street, shop and restaurant names so that I could verify where I'd been. About 30 minutes later I floated back into my body. I wrote down every detail of what happened and then drove through the streets I had flown over. Everything was exactly as I'd seen out of my body.

After this, I had many OBEs, usually when I was in a drowsy, half-asleep, half-awake state early in the morning. I never met Masters in the Himalayas or Indian gurus on the banks of the Ganges, but I did zap about at the speed of light between many different countries, usually pricing tomatoes in local markets. Although out of my body, I never moved beyond the Earth plane. However, I did experience an expansion of consciousness that enabled me to do, see and know things I could not have done with my physical senses.

Another type of OBE, described as 'bilocation', is when a person travels out of their body to a certain place and is reported to have been seen there at the same time as others know they were in their own house or with them.

An extraordinary example of this ability was Padre Pio, a Capuchin monk, who had the power to appear in several places at once. In one incident during the First World War, General Cardona, who had suffered a defeat, was in his tent contemplating suicide. A young monk entered his tent and said, 'Come, General, you would not do anything so stupid.' At the end of the war, the General heard so much talk about Padre Pio that he went to his church in Foggia, Italy, and, to his amazement, recognized him as the young monk who had saved him from suicide. Alberto del Faute, Padre Pio's biographer, describes many more such incidents.

In the past, the ability to project out of the physical body was commonplace, taught in ancient mystery schools and practised by shamans, magicians and occultists. In the future everyone will know how to move in and out of the body with ease. In fact

Robert Monroe, the American pioneer of journeys out of the body and author of a book of the same name, before his death in 1996 developed a unique programme called 'Going Home', which teaches people who face imminent death – whether from terminal illness or old age – how to leave their bodies at will and so overcome any fear of the act of dying.

Rose, a blind woman I know, learned how to pop out of her body after attending classes on psychic development. She used to project herself to hotels she and her husband stayed in on holiday two or three weeks before the holiday began to make sure she knew where the furniture was placed in their bedroom. Out of her body she could see perfectly well. On one occasion the porter led her to a different room from the one booked, thinking, 'She's blind and will not know the difference.' To his amazement, Rose insisted on having the room they'd booked, 'Because everything in this room is in the wrong place.'

Imagine how wonderful it would be for all blind, paralysed, crippled or bedridden people if they could learn to project themselves beyond the restrictions imposed by their physical disabilities.

The basic requirement for astral travel and out-of-body experience is the belief that it is possible. The second is the will to do it. In my own case, the harder I tried, the harder it became. Yet when I gave up, relaxed and stopped trying, it happened by itself. Deep relaxation, visualization and meditation can all help trigger an OBE. Sylvan Muldoon, co-author of *The Projection of the Astral Body*, suggests that imagining going to the top of a very high building in a lift as you lie down to sleep can induce OBEs as well as astral travel. Always invoke love, light and protection before you do this.

During out-of-body journeys, astral travel and lucid dreams we sometimes see our own body as if it was someone else. Don Juan, Carlos Castaneda's teacher, calls this the 'third gate of dreaming', and says that once we have seen ourselves asleep we must learn to move our energy or light body around. The easiest way to do this is to will it to move, in a gliding, floating motion rather than to step forward as if in a physical body.

The dreams or sleep state experiences described in this chapter are an avenue through which we can familiarize ourselves with out-of-body states and make contact with our higher or soul selves. Once we have sensed this level of consciousness our outlook on life changes dramatically. We literally move from self – to cosmic consciousness.

DREAMS OF OTHER WORLDS

Who looks outside dreams;
Who looks inside wakes.

C.G. JUNG

DEATH AND DYING

Many people fear that the death of someone in a dream means that the person will die in waking life. Yet death dreams seldom predict literal, physical death. Rather, they give us a nudge to change, to grow, to release, or 'die to' certain habits, relationships, emotions or even work that no longer serves our need to develop, as well as to old ways of living and perceiving life. So, a dream of death is a symbol or metaphor for letting go of, or transforming, an aspect of ourselves as well as an acknowledgement that something inside us may be dead.

For example, Joe, a solidly built, tough-talking, hard-working lorry driver, dreamed he was in a cemetery digging around an unmarked grave. He dug deeply and finally dragged out of the ground an old coffin, which he opened. Inside was a beautiful but fragile woman, who looked more asleep than dead. Shocked, Joe knew he must lift her out onto the grass and revive her. As he did so, he awoke. Discussing the dream later, Joe realized he was so macho-minded that he had buried, and was dead to, his feminine side. The dream was positive in the sense that Joe *knew* he must revive the woman and attempted to do so.

Another coffin dream illustrating the death of freedom, spontaneity and movement was that of Bill, who dreamed he was hammering nails into a wooden coffin which had his name inscribed on it. Anticipating imminent death, and worried about his family's future, he made a will. Months later, exhausted from the pressure of his job, which literally 'boxed him in', Bill remembered his dream and realized his workaholic attitude to life was nailing him into a position where there was no life, no room to breathe. Neither Joe's nor Bill's dream had anything to do with physical death.

Often death dreams show a friend, neighbour or acquaintance being knocked over by a 10 ton truck, struck by lightning or falling off a mountain. As Ashleigh Brilliant once said, 'I could accept death more easily if I could be sure it only happened to other people.' Certainly, it is usually easier to see an accident befall another person rather than ourselves. But what do these dreams mean? Although they can occasionally be predictive, they also mean we must look at what the person in our dream symbolizes, or represents, to us in our waking life. If we witness their death in a dream, we must question what needs to die in us, as well as our own attitude to death and the process of dying.

Many of us in the West fear death or the act of dying, and as people age and their bodies become more frail and susceptible to illness and accident, dreams of death are common. These are obviously different from the type of death dream that illustrates change in the physical world.

Characteristic dreams of older people who are near death – from age rather than illness – are generally of loss: the loss of a purse, passport, wallet or handbag, for example. These all

symbolize the loss of identity. Other common dream themes of approaching death in older people are of funerals, journeys, seeing themselves in coffins or attending their own funeral, or of white birds, beautiful gardens, celebrations and flower-filled villages or houses.

Ann Ree Colton, whose dreamwork I mentioned earlier, says that black water, a tuberose, a skeleton, a funeral and a brown skull in a dream all warn of physical death. A white skull, a coffin, a casket and a cold wind symbolize death to one's desires and wishes, death to the material world, the fear of death and the old life. She also says that a black horse, a tree with dead limbs, or one that is covered with ice and snow warn of physical death, as does a tree on fire, whereas to dream of a black pearl shows an unconscious fascination with death. In my own dreamwork I found that to flee from death in a dream means we are avoiding an inner prompting to change.

Change is also the significance of the death dreams of healthy children, which often include the death of their parents. Such dreams are connected to growth, discovery and moving from one phase to another. Parents who dream of their children's death (when they are healthy) are not only reminded to look at their own inner child (see also page 118) but also to let go of their physical children as they grow up. These dreams are sometimes the result of conscious or unconscious resistance to do so.

The dreams of children on the verge of death are amazingly lucid and preparatory for their release from the physical body. Katie dreamed she crossed a riverbed while her parents remained on the other side. When they tried to join her, she waved them back and walked into a beautiful garden where many other children were playing and dancing. Nine-year-old David, chronically ill with leukaemia, dreamed that he arrived on Earth by floating down in a balloon. A childhood friend, killed in a car accident three years earlier, then appeared and handed David a bunch of multi-coloured balloons. He said, 'When you want to use these balloons to float back to where we come from, I'll be waiting for you.' Suddenly David saw hundreds of children, all holding balloons, floating in the air around him. He awoke excited and happy at the thought of joining them. Both dreams enabled these two children to float away without fear, panic or pain when the moment of death came.

While most death dreams symbolize change and transformation rather than actual loss of life, some can also prepare us for death – our own and others. Jenny had a recurring dream in which her sister Mary opened a door in a wall and walked into a beautiful garden. As Jenny approached the door, Mary began to gently close it in her face, allowing Jenny only the briefest glimpse of masses of flowers, radiant with colour and light. Upset at Mary's refusal to share the beauty with her, Jenny usually woke up. About 18 months after the dreams began, Mary had a massive heart attack and died instantly.

Although Jenny was deeply upset, she realized her recurring dream had in some way prepared her for Mary to go off on her own into a place where Jenny could not follow. Two years later, the dreams re-occurred but now, as Jenny approached the door, it opened wide and she could see a garden of unbelievable beauty. Huge trees, emerald green grass, flowers of every colour and description, splashing fountains, streams and pools, exotic birds and animals, as well as ducks and rabbits, filled her gaze. Awed by the beauty, Jenny usually awoke. After four or five of these dreams, she was diagnosed as having cancer. Although she did everything she could to recover, her dreams gave her a peaceful understanding that it was her time to go, and so she did.

Tibetan Buddhists believe that each time we sleep we experience the condition of our soul in dreams, and if we were to die in our sleep, we would simply continue the dream we were having.

Alice Bailey wrote:

> 'The process of daily sleep and the process of occasional dying are identical, with one difference, that in sleep the magnetic thread or current of energy along which the life-force streams is preserved intact and constitutes the path of return to the body. In death this life thread is broken or snaps.'

In other words, we should not fear death but accept it as an inevitable part of life. Death is a birth into another reality. Birth is a death from another reality.

Private Dowding, a soldier, described his death to Wellesley Tudor-Pole who, amongst other things, developed Chalice Well in Glastonbury. Tudor-Pole channelled this information from Dowding:

> 'Physical death is nothing. There is really no cause for fear … This is what happened. I have a perfectly clear memory of the whole incident. I was waiting at the corner of a traverse to go on guard. It was a fine evening. I had no special intimation of danger until I heard the whizz of a shell. There followed an explosion somewhere behind me. I crouched down, but it was too late … I fell, and as I did so, without passing through any apparent interval of unconsciousness, I found myself outside myself … You will know what a small incident dying is …'

We can invoke dreams to prepare ourselves for death and free ourselves from the fear of it, thereby enabling ourselves to live life more fully. In fact dreams help us adjust to *this* world by providing a bridge or a lifeline to the next. When Plato was on his deathbed he was asked what was the most important message he wanted to leave behind for humanity. He replied: 'Practise to die.'

If you fear the act of dying, write down every detail of the worst death you can imagine. Burn it. Then write down every detail of the best death you can imagine. Keep it and read it from time to time. In this way you reprogramme your subconscious not to fear death.

Another way to overcome the fear of death is to spend time with a person who *is* dying. Dying patients are usually shunted away as if dying were a contagious disease. But it is when we are dying that we need love, touch and honest communication most of all. To sit and hold the hand of a dying person, with absolute love, is a life-changing experience which heals all fear. In one of his workshops, Dannion Brinkley, author of *Peace in the Light*, said, 'Be with a person taking their first breath, and their last. When you find someone who has nothing to give you back, except love, you find yourself.'

DREAMS OF UFOS AND ETS

We live in very exciting times and what will probably turn out to be one of the most dramatic and potent periods of change in the history of mankind. Global communication gives us instant information on events occurring a million miles away. Satellites in outer space reveal that planets such as Mars may have supported not just life but a highly advanced civilization.

The mass media increasingly focuses on unusual phenomena such as UFO sightings, the world-wide appearance of crop circles, solar flares, dramatic changes in the weather, the Photon belt (an interdimensional band or envelope of light discovered in 1961) and their possible effect on our lives, as well as men and women who claim contact with, and even abduction by, aliens.

Today we do not raise an eyebrow when we read reports of comets such as the Hale-Bopp (discovered in July 1995 by Alan Hale and Thomas Bopp), gamma rays, ozone holes, quarks, neutrons, protons, photons, stellar explosions, galaxies, black holes, quasars and supernovae. Astronauts and cosmonauts who land on the moon and study the stars from space stations suspended in the sky are no longer subjects of intense curiosity, but rather stimulate hundreds of people to envision inter-planetary vacations in the not so distant future.

In the 1500s, the French doctor Nostradamus, one of the greatest mystics and prophets ever known, predicted that the end of the millenium would bring great upheavals, including holes in the ozone layer, global warming, black holes, earthquakes and spacecraft crashes, while the philosopher Sir George Trevelyan once said that what is taking place now is 'the greatest revolution in the intellectual climate of human thought. We are discovering that this planet is not just one tiny, unimportant speck in the universe, nor are we the only civilization ...'

In his book *The Undiscovered Self*, Jung wrote, 'Humans will not know who we are until we make contact with quasi-human mammals from another star' and hundreds of books and movies have not only opened people's minds to the possibility of UFOs and extra-terrestial communication but have also made the idea increasingly popular.

It has been suggested that much technology used by the mythical ancient civilization of Atlantis came from outer space. Some descriptions suggest that men like gods flew through the air, over and under the sea, across and through the Earth, and taught the Atlanteans how to harness the energy of the sun through giant and carefully placed crystals. They used the resulting rays for heat and light, the development of psychic powers, the rejuvenation of ailing bodies, the transport of huge objects and the invention of atomic power. Because this energy was finally misused, enormous explosions were set off, devastating the land and resulting in the end of the Atlantean civilization. Many psychics, including Edgar Cayce, have predicted that parts of Atlantis will rise out of the sea before the end of the century and that the area in and around the Bermuda Triangle is where a major Atlantean crystal lies buried.

Most indigenous people believe they came from the stars – the Australian Aboriginals, for example, trace themselves back to a race from the constellation known as the Seven Sisters, or Pleiades. They say they are still in communication with their brothers in the sky and await their arrival to help reshape the world. Many African tribes also believe they were seeded from outer space. Until fairly recently, many dismissed such ideas as ridiculous. Now, after such carefully researched books such as *Fingerprints of the Gods, Keeper of Genesis, The Orion Mystery, The Sirius Mystery* and the writings of von Däniken and Velikovsky, together with dramatic sightings of UFOs and supposed messages from outer space, even scientists are willing to take a second look.

In addition to claims by numerous people that they have had joy-rides in spacecraft and have many extra-terrestial friends from other planets, there are also a number of men and women who claim to be psychic channels of information fed to them telepathically from outer space. Many of the messages purport to come from the Pleiadians, who tell us that when the Photon belt merges fully with the Earth, it will move our solar system into a higher dimension, with the result that humans will live in the reality of galactic light. The Pleiadians say that Photon energy will transform our DNA and chakra systems, restore us to full consciousness (including the memory of who we are and where we came from) and, by ending our dependence on fuel, will allow us to travel through space. Apparently starships are

operated by Photon power, or the power of light. The Pleiadians claim that they are here to promote humans into higher consciousness and to help birth a new human spirit so that Earth can reclaim its relationship with other galactic beings spread across the galaxy.

While many people believe that throughout history inter-galactic intelligence has communicated with mankind (sometimes in forms described as angels) today's avalanche of information, from both incarnate and discarnate sources, has stimulated a massive shift in human awareness. We are rapidly waking up to our relationship to every facet of life, human and non-human, that exists both on and beyond this Earth. We are becoming part of a new species, a new culture. Instead of stepping out of the water onto land, we are lifting from the Earth into the sky – moving from self-consciousness to cosmic consciousness.

It is therefore, no wonder that UFOs, interplanetary exploration and meetings with ETs are increasingly common in our dreams.

When living in America, I came across the work of Sherry and Brad Steiger, the authors of many books and long-time researchers into UFO phenomena. Both Sherry and Brad claim contact with what they call 'multi-dimensional beings from outer space', which they say changed their perception of life on Earth and the universe as a whole. They say that anyone who experiences particularly vivid dreams of UFOs and ETs may be having contact with extra-terrestial intelligence while they sleep. Amongst the data the Steigers and other UFO researchers have compiled from people who claim UFO dreams and experiences are physical symptoms such as an unexplained hole in the eardrum or puncture mark/s in the navel, sore eyes, swollen joints, sinusitis, strange scars and skin rashes. They also describe dreams of flying, viewing the Earth from another

planet, being taught or examined by small or unusual people and the sense of climbing aboard or being drawn into a UFO as typical of UFO/ET experience.

Although I can lay claim to sore eyes, swollen joints, sinusitis, strange scars and skin rashes, as well as puncture marks around my navel – though not all at the same time – I do not believe I myself have had any extra-terrestrial contact. As a result of guided imagery, however, I did once have a very powerful dream in which an androgenous figure without ears, clad in a skintight silver outfit which included a close-fitting skull cap, led me to a temple in the stars, in which I was shown my book of life and how to use it.

A few years ago, because I met a number of people who either claimed to have communication with UFO beings or to have been kidnapped by them, I believed I was being prepared for contact. Unfortunately this never happened, despite hours of sitting on mountain tops at times of full and new moons and gazing at strange cloud formations in the sky …

During a seminar in New Zealand, I met Chris, who told me that for 10 years he dreamed every night of a woman who spoke to him from another planet. She insisted he was not of this Earth and constantly reminded him of his 'beyond the stars' identity. Chris lived for his dreams, until finally, the woman told him he was too involved with her teachings (which had inspired him to pass school and university exams) and that he must now fully participate with life on Earth. She said 'We will now cut the contact,' and did so.

Chris was so devastated that he had a nervous breakdown from which it took him two years to recover. The dreams never returned.

At the time the dreams began, Chris's mother had found a square bald patch on his head, and accused him of deliberately ruining an expensive haircut. To this day the hair has never

grown back. Two or three other people, whose stories of UFO contact I believe, have also shown me square bald patches behind the ears.

If you wish to encourage UFO dreams, I suggest you read as much as you can on the subject and see as many 'contact'-type movies as possible. When you go to bed, having done one or two of the relaxation exercises described earlier (see pages 19–22), visualize yourself entering a golden yellow globe or a huge crystal ball and imagine floating away to the moon, or a planet such as Mars or Venus.

A good visualization exercise is to image floating or swimming through the stars far above the Earth and drifting down to land on each planet in turn. Imagine the surface of the moon and the sensation of your bare feet in contact with it. Take time to look around and examine the landscape. Notice the vegetation and any people or buildings. Do not force the moon to appear as you see it in photos, but allow your inner senses to reveal it to you. Take time to explore and then imagine a moon maiden advancing to greet you. What is she wearing? Does she walk or float a little above the ground? Does she have anything on her head? How do you feel as she reaches you? Does she speak verbally or telepathically? What would she like you to know about life on the moon? What would she like to know about you and life on Earth? When you feel ready to leave, imagine that she hands you a gift which is symbolic of an energy or talent you can use on Earth. Take it and thank her. Maybe there is something you would like to give in return. If so, do so now – or suggest that you will bring a gift from Earth on your next visit. Gradually lift off and up, or re-enter your globe or crystal.

You may want to stop there and drift into sleep, or you may like to continue your journey by landing on Mars. Let Mars unfold before your inner eye and then imagine a Martian approaching you and proceed in a similar way as you did with the moon maiden. Again, receive a gift, symbolic of Martian energy, to use in your life on Earth. After this, and before returning to Earth, you may want to visit Venus. Let yourself feel and imagine every aspect of what interests you here and when you meet a Venusian you will also be presented with a gift.

You can do this with any of the planets, either each one as a separate visualization or two or three one after the other. It is better not to visit a dozen planets in the same exercise, as you do not assimilate the experience fully. Now, in your mind's eye, return to your bed and sleep. If you use this exercise during the day, always remember to ground yourself properly afterwards.

Other ways to stimulate UFO dreams are pre-sleep:

1) Write a letter and ask your angels and guides to introduce you to an ET in a dream or to take you to a particular galaxy where you may see some.
2) Mentally send out a message into the universe asking for an ET to appear in a dream.
3) Awake, but with closed eyes, imagine an ET appearing in front of you. What would it look like? Say to you? Ask you to do? How could it help you? What could it teach you? Mentally ask any questions you want and listen for answers that may pop into your mind as words, symbols or shapes.
4) Meditate during times of new and full moons, equinoxes and solstices.
5) Meditate on the moon's entry into different zodiac signs – silently ask yourself how does the moon in Scorpio feel in comparison to the moon in Gemini, for example.

The more spiritual work you can do on yourself, the greater the likelihood of these exercises working because your vibrational frequency will be higher and finer.

Always remember to ask for the protection of God, and your angels or guides, and that *only* outer space beings who are of absolute love, truth, goodness and higher awareness make contact.

Like angels, ETs will appear in the form most acceptable to you and not necessarily as a one-eyed, or bug-eyed, androgynous, foetus-like figure. Two people I spoke to who claim ET contact described tall blond young men in black leather. Although they lived in completely different parts of the world and never met, each mentioned the strangely luminous tawny eyes and instant, magical materialization and dematerialization of the two men.

Like all pre-sleep dream preparation, these exercises need practice, so unless you are lucky, you may not have an extra-terrestial visitor in your dreams immediately. A group of friends who formed a small dream club in order to do in-depth work on their dreams practised some of these exercises and after six months still had no UFO experience. However, they began to receive messages from some sort of inter-planetary council who called themselves the Ashtar Command. When the club members began to apply some of the information they received to their waking lives, they found that both their health and ability to handle problems improved dramatically.

PAST LIVES

Many of the current challenges in our lives, whether in the form of stressful relationships, fears, addictions, physical disabilities or feelings of worthlessness and self-doubt, can be faced and successfully overcome by looking at the past lives, as well as the past years of *this* life, that set them in motion.

For a number of people, the idea of reincarnation is ridiculous. Current research, however, suggests that two thirds of the world's population believe in past and future lives. For them it makes absolute sense to think of the Earth plane as a school, offering a billion choices of experience ranging from simple kindergarten-type challenges to opportunities and lessons of university degree quality. We do not expect children to remain in kindergarten – as each year passes, they move on, acquiring greater knowledge and self-confidence as they do so. In a similar way, for soul growth, each life provides myriad new experiences on our journey towards wisdom and enlightenment.

To develop spiritual understanding, or enlightenment, requires many lifetimes, both as a male and a female. These lifetimes must include every facet of human event and emotion: doubt, fear, hate, birth, death, sickness, rejection, sorrow, loss, despair, jealousy and punishment, as well as joy, love, power, success, health and happiness. As the wise old gull said to Jonathon in Richard Bach's *Jonathan Livingston Seagull*,

> 'Do you have any idea how many lives we must have gone through before we even got the first idea that there is more to life than eating, or fighting, or power in the flock? A thousand lives, Jon, ten thousand. And then another hundred lives until we begin to learn there is such a thing as perfection, and another hundred again to get the idea that our purpose for living is to find that perfection and show it forth. The same rule holds for us now, of course; we choose our next world through what we learn in this one.'

I have always believed in reincarnation because I grew up seeing past, present and future simultaneously. A person's face in front of me would suddenly dissolve into another face of a different race, sex and era. Sometimes six or eight different faces would emerge from the person I was looking at. It was often confusing. I not only saw the past, present and future of the people around me, but also of the trees, houses, bricks and stones. However, until I spontaneously recalled a number of my own past lives that shed light on certain events, relationships, health factors, fears and other problems, I never recognized the power of the past to affect our lives in the present.

Since then, in fact for over 25 years, I have used regression or past-life therapy in all my counselling and therapeutic sessions. Even people who do not believe in reincarnation have surprised themselves by successfully overcoming problems in this way.

In the 1950s *The Search for Bridie Murphy*, a book about an American housewife who under hypnosis claimed to remember a life in eighteenth-century Ireland, created enormous controversy. Since then, numerous books and stories have caused an explosion of interest in the idea of reincarnation and past-life recall. This interest includes that of doctors, psychiatrists and psychologists, many of whom discovered that patients suffering from a variety of symptoms previously 'unresponsive to treatment' recovered, often instantly, on recalling the life in which the problem originated. As Dr J. B. Rhine, director of psychology at Duke University in America, said, 'The psychology of today looks at the mind of today. The psychology of tomorrow will look at the past.'

A number of doctors now echo the sentiments of Denys Kelsey, the psychiatrist husband of Joan Grant, who wrote extraordinary novels based on her own past-life memories. Dr Kelsey commented, 'I should like people to believe in my belief in reincarnation. I think it would cause them to be much happier, much less frightened and more sane.'

The basic principle of past-life therapy is to extricate from a person's unconscious and subconscious feelings and memories that stem from the past. Usually the mere reliving of them in the mind and imagination will dissipate them. This applies just as much to memories of early childhood and other years of this present life as to any other.

Past-life therapy deals with the root cause of a problem rather than a symptom and, as Morris Netherton, another doctor, says, 'It allows you to start doing things with people because you want to and not because you have to.'

There are as many ways to reconnect to the memories that can cause a hiccup in our ability to cope easily with life as there are foods on a restaurant menu. These include meditation, visualization, body-work, journal-writing, drawing, astrology, numerology, runes, Tarot, the *I Ching*, past-life therapy, and aura and chakra reading. However, many of these techniques are subject to the personal interpretation of an outside 'reader' in a way that dreams are not.

The therapist Eno van Waveren, a student of Jung's in the 1930s, said that the only way to check the proof of reincarnation is through dreams: 'They are the only proof we have – the dream is the taproot.' Van Waveren wrote a book, *Pilgrimage to Re-Birth*, in which he describes some of the lives revealed to him through dreams, going back to 700 BC.

A fascinating example of the power of past-life dreams to affect life in the present is the story of Dorothy Eady, an Englishwoman who had recurring dreams about Egypt and her relationship with the Pharoah Sety. Dorothy's dreams introduced her to reincarnation, astral travel and life in Aneuti, the land of the dead. She finally moved to Egypt and unofficially resumed her duties as a priestess of Isis, which,

according to her dreams, she had been 3,000 years ago. She became known as Omm Sety, which means 'Mother of Sety' in Arabic, although in the past she had actually been Sety's lover, not his mother.

Omm Sety was consumed by her dreams and inspired by her unshakeable belief in what they revealed. She lived them out in a way that enriched her life rather than cut her off from it. We can follow her example and use past-life dreams to gain greater understanding of where some of our blocks, personality traits and relationships (good and bad) originated.

In my experience, to ask a dream for information about previous lives has always brought a response, not only for me, but for others too. The key to success with any kind of past-life therapy, especially in dreams, is the real *need* to know, rather than idle curiosity. Curiosity may provide the original stimulus, but need provides a stronger, deeper motive. For example, I may need to understand and forgive my parents, release repressed emotions which hold me back from living a full and happy life or discover why I stifle my creativity. If I am addicted to drugs, alcohol, power, success or failure and misery, and I want to overcome the addiction, I need to know the original cause. (Any kind of addiction is a form of emotional suppression, usually the result of chronic patterns of self-hate and self-criticism that can create such stress the immune system is weakened.) If I *need* to know why, for example, out of my five children, one is so difficult and unresponsive to any kind of affection, while the others love a hug or a cuddle, I am far more likely to get an answer than if I merely speculate on whether I was Cleopatra or the Queen of Sheba in another life.

Occasionally, a person will fear what they may discover but in my own life and in my own work, I have found that no memory reveals itself until or unless the time is right.

There appears to be an inbuilt safety mechanism in our consciousness which protects us from knowing too much before we are able to deal with, and use, the knowledge to improve the quality of this present life. Another fear may be that a past-life dream is only an imaginary fantasy. However, when a dream 'hits', the emotional, physical and mental reaction is quite different from the reaction to a fantasy. Just as when we 'know' someone is telling us a lie, so we 'know' when a past-life image is true or false.

A past-life therapist will initially guide their subject into a state of deep relaxation before asking questions that stimulate past-life recall. To encourage dreams of previous lives, we need to follow the same format but in reverse. In other words, write down, or speak into a tape-recorder, the questions you want answered *before* you relax. Do not ask for a dream that covers everything at once. Focus on the problem, situation, event or personality that you need information about, one at a time. Ask questions in your own way, but also think of a country or period in history you feel drawn to or revulsed by. If anything in your life today stimulates extraordinary emotion, think of how this affects you and question where it came from. Use dreams of the past to connect you to your purpose in life, the major lessons you came here to learn, why you chose the physical, mental and emotional bodies you have at this time, and where your relationship with your parents came from. Ask for dreams that reveal to you your journey from conception to birth, childhood to adulthood. Present life and prenatal regression are just as important as regression into other lives and can make deeper journeys into the past much easier.

If you have questions about certain people in your life, imagine asking them 'Where did I know you before?' while you hold an image of their face and eyes in your mind's eye before sleep.

To relax, follow any of the pre-sleep exercises given earlier, and for people who hate the idea of any form of exercise, no matter how simple, I suggest you visualize doing it.

Gandhi once said, 'It's nature's kindness that we don't remember past births,' but in today's world, to remember, accept and release crucial events from the past can lead to total transformation of our present lives.

No matter what kind of dream I want to invoke, I always ask that only that which is for my highest good may be revealed to me. I also ask that only that which is of God, good, love and truth be present and that anything inappropriate to my consciousness may be released. Whether I do this before sleep or meditation, I say think you afterwards.

DREAM INCUBATION AND VISION QUESTS

'Crying for a vision, that's the beginning of all religion. The thirst for a dream from above – without this, you are nothing,' said Lone Deer, a Native American who was appalled at the empty desert white men create within themselves when they no longer cry for a dream.

Vision quests and dream incubation are similar in the sense that both are powerful ways of asking questions and receiving answers. However, a vision quest, usually practised by indigenous people, especially the Native Americans, is embarked on primarily to discover a person's life task and the animal which will be his guiding spirit, whereas dream incubation was practised in the past by priests, priestesses and the sick as a means of invoking the gods to heal through dreams and visions.

The priests, priestesses, wise men and magicians of ancient Greece and Egypt were highly trained in the use of ritual, ceremony and spiritual discipline as part of the preparation for inducing god-inspired dreams. They purified themselves, fasted, prayed, recited special formulae and dozens of incantations to ward off evil and give protection during sleep.

The Egyptians assimilated a great deal of their attitude to dreams from other societies and civilizations. In turn, the Greeks borrowed heavily from the Egyptians, so many of their rituals in which incense, drugs, herbs, hypnotic exercises, fasting and magic spells were used were very similar. Like the Egyptians, the Greeks believed that dreams and fantasy – the word comes from the Greek *phantasia*, which means 'to imagine', 'to make visible the invisible' or 'to reveal' – were the means by which the gods spoke to man. It was through *phantasia* that dreams occurred, so the Greeks did everything they could to stimulate it. Ceremonies to arouse the imagination and induce a sense of euphoria included art, music, movement, dance, acting and mime, which were as important as the use of herbs, incense and intoxicating drugs.

Today the use of drugs and intoxicants is considered to be a social evil, an escape from reality that, if abused, can deaden our feelings and cut us from life. In the past, however, priests, priestesses, teachers, shamans and holy men both took and administered a variety of drugs, including alcohol, during prescribed religious ceremonies. Instead of cutting them off from life, the dreams, visions and fantasies that resulted were a source of growth, wisdom, strength and renewal.

To invoke or incubate a dream within a temple was a sacred rite requiring intense preliminary work which was a prime cause of the dynamic results obtained by those who embarked upon it. To start with, admission to the healing temples was forbidden unless one was invited to enter by the god of healing himself, in a dream. In ancient Greece, as already mentioned, Asklepios was the god of healing. His symbol was a snake and even today the caduceus – two snakes coiled round a staff – is an international sign for medicine. Asklepios really existed around 1100 BC and was a man for whom dreams were the foundation of physical, psychic and spiritual growth and health. His work laid the foundation for the use of dream incubation in temples and sacred sites as a major source of healing for centuries after his death.

In order to gain admission to the healing temples a sick person would consult the oracles and soothsayers, purify him- or herself with herbs, make pilgrimages to holy sites and make sacrifices to the gods long before invoking Asklepios' help. After all this, if he was fortunate enough to have Asklepios appear in a dream, he had to describe it in detail to the temple priests. If they believed his dream genuine he was allowed into the outer temple, in which long hours were spent in prayer and solitude, sleeping under the rays of the moon, bathing in springs and streams, fasting, or undergoing a strict diet. Physical exercise, the inhalation of herbs, and the witnessing of profound musical and dramatic performances were all encouraged to relax the mind and body. It was believed that when someone was completely relaxed – in a semi-trance or even in a state of ecstasy – the spirit was more likely to have a vision or mystical experience.

After days – sometimes even weeks and months – of lengthy preparation, the sick person was expected to have a second dream in which Asklepios now invited him into the inner temple where the real healing took place. He was also expected to make a sacrificial offering to the priests. If his circumstances were comfortable, he would give a goat or sheep, if not he would give honey or herbs. Once inside the temple, the lights were dimmed and the sick person lay on a mat or the still warm skin of the sacrificed animal and listened to the scuffle of the sacred temple snakes slithering over the floor and the rustle and breathing of the people around him. Apprehensive and disoriented by all he had seen and done, fully expectant of a dream or vision to cure him, it is no wonder that he often experienced miraculous healings and dreams.

Dream incubation rites had the same effect as hypnotic or auto-suggestion might have on us today. The priests were true physicians who understood that health involved the integration of mind, body, spirit and emotion, unlike many modern doctors, who treat each part separately.

Ritualistic preparations for a vision quest can be compared to those for dream incubation. They, too, are designed to cleanse and purify the body, heighten the senses and stimulate such a strong expectation that a dream or vision will manifest that it usually does.

While each Native American tribe has rites unique to its own tradition, the vision quest seems common to all. So, too, does the reverence for nature, the acknowledgement of the oneness of all life and the different prayers and greetings to every animal, bird, bush, tree, stone, rock, star, stream and flower – in fact everything on and in the Earth and everything above and beyond it, all of which are loved and accepted as relatives. According to Luther Standing Bear, a Dakota Sioux in the Dakota tradition, children were taught never to fear nature because everything, in its own way, communicated to them in the same way as their families did at home. Indeed, one aspect of the vision quest is to deepen a person's spiritual understanding of nature and its mysteries.

Because an individual vision quest is a sacred rite of passage that initiates a boy child into adulthood and enables him to discover his particular mission in life and therefore his place in the tribe or community, the first quest usually takes place around puberty. Although Native American children, like most indigenous people, are brought up to value dreams and to expect to undergo the quest at adolescence, it can still be a scary experience.

A Native American friend of mine described the apprehension of waiting for three or four days for a vision which he feared might never come. Before he entered the vision pit – a pit dug under the earth and covered with branches, grass or leaves – he had spent days fasting and meditating in solitude before joining his father and uncles in a sweat lodge ceremony. Purified by the aromatic smoke of burning sage, his mind loose, as if the strings attaching him to everyday life were melting away in the heat of the fire pit and the scalding steam that arose when icy water was thrown onto it, light-headed from inhaling tobacco from the sacred pipe for the first time, now cold and alone in the vision pit, my friend prayed not only for a vision, but that he would also survive the night. Most adolescent boys undergo this initiation naked and without food or water, although some tribes allow them a blanket. Their cry for a vision is a true cry, for without an answer, or an indication from the ancestors and animal spirits, a boy will have no proper place in the tribe. In the case of this friend, it took about four days before his dreams and vision became so clear it was as if he was in a different reality. During these four days he lost all sense of time, his body became numb with cold, he was very thirsty and the atmosphere around him was charged with shadowy animal and human shapes that brushed past him, causing shivers down his spine. After his quest was over, he realized he was no longer a child, but a man, ready to assume his responsibilities within the tribe.

Many of us today, trying to juggle job, family, house, finances, etc., may feel resistant to the idea of elaborate dream incubation rites and even more resistant to sitting naked in the local park while we undergo our own personal vision quest. Nevertheless, the basic principles of asking for help, healing or insight, preparing oneself, sleeping in a sacred or peaceful place, and reverence for the whole process, are as valid for us who live in the cities and suburbs as for the ancient Greeks and Native Americans.

For 12 years, one of my own adopted practices was to spend four or five weeks camping and climbing in the Rila Mountains of Bulgaria with a group of Beinsa Douna's students. We slept in tiny primitive tents, with wind, rain and snow sometimes blowing in, and climbed to the highest mountain peak at 3.30 a.m. to greet the sun. It was usually pitch dark when we set off and I never thought I would survive to the top. We put questions – sometimes silently in prayer, sometimes written on scraps of paper and left under a stone – to the Sphinx, a huge black rock that marked the top of our ascent. Completely cut off from the rest of the world, we danced the Paneurhythmy, a sacred dance that aligns body, mind and spirit, prayed, walked dreamed, meditated, climbed, searched for wood and water, and survived on basic provisions of bread (stone-hard after a month), tomatoes and cheese, plus honey-filled hot water with herbs, gathered as we climbed. Terrified of some of the heights, isolated and without food for 24 hours at a time on a number of occasions, due to snow and ice freezing us into our tents, I felt stripped of all connection to the outside world. Information about past, present and future poured into my head, and was frequently confirmed by another member of the group a few days later.

The power of dream incubation and vision quest comes from the idea or belief that solitude and suffering open the mind and true wisdom can only be found away from others. For me, my Bulgarian experiences proved the truth of this, but we can all incorporate these ideas into everyday life without such extreme measures.

The most simple way to incubate a dream is to write a question down and literally sleep on it by putting it under your pillow. Another is to write the question down in tiny writing on a small piece of paper and stick this, with Sellotape or elastoplast, to the centre of your forehead, affirming it verbally as you go to bed. The more preparation you put into this, the more powerful the result is likely to be.

Dependant on where you live, any of the following, when done with an attitude of conscious preparation, can substitute as a sweat lodge – although of course the real thing is much better. To take a sauna, a Turkish bath, to sit in hot springs, float on the waters of the Dead Sea or in a Samadhi tank (sometimes called a floatation tank), to shower or soak in a hot ginger bath at home can all help release mental, emotional and physical toxins as well as produce a slightly altered state of consciousness.

My recipe for the ginger bath is to throw two heaped tablespoons of dry powdered ginger (not fresh) into a bath or tub of hot water and soak in it, up to your neck, for as long as you can, keeping it as hot as you can bear it without burning yourself. Make sure you have a warm towel to wrap yourself in afterwards and go straight to bed. This is *not* a beauty treatment but a form of therapy, so it is inadvisable to do it in the morning. The combination of ginger and hot water draws tension from the muscles and negativity – such as chronic tiredness, old emotions or shock – from the auric field. This can result in tears, anger or nausea, which are all good signs of release, but we need to allow ourselves the overnight space to recover. Aside from using a ginger bath myself as a preparation for dream incubation, I also immerse myself in one after months of travel and workshopping. It is *not* something to do every day.

Many of the suggestions given in Chapter Three, such as aura cleansing and creating a special or sacred space in which to sleep, can also be used before incubating a dream. Herbal smudge sticks and incense are usually available in alternative health or alternative book shops. If you cannot find any, buy a bunch of dried herbs, light them just enough to smoulder and brush yourself and your room with the smoke. If this does not appeal, simply open your bedroom window and then go around the room clapping your hands sharply together while you say words to the effect of 'I command anything not appropriate to my consciousness to be gone. Only that which is of God and love may remain.' Imagine any negativity floating out of the window before you close it – or leave it open.

Candles, flowers (especially roses), plants, crystals and stones, favourite objects or colours, handmade glass, mirrors, pictures that you either love or are inspired by, all help to create a sacred atmosphere in a room.

Physical preparation could include exercise, massage (of feet, hands or full body), long walks, leaning against a tree, swimming in the sea – anything that puts you in touch with nature – as well as a fast. My first fast lasted three days. I ate nothing but drank vast quantities of water. Afterwards I felt mentally clear, physically light and emotionally full. If the thought of fasting horrifies you, consider a one-day cleansing diet of juice or fruit or a fast that starts after lunch and continues until supper the following day. In this way you do eat, but give your body a 24-hour break from digesting food.

Always drink lots of liquid when you do this – but no coffee, tea or alcohol.

You do not have to follow all of these suggestions at once. You may want to take a few days or weeks to prepare, especially if you have reached a crossroads in your life and are seeking answers about where to go next.

When you feel ready to incubate your dream, write down your question on paper and also write your own, waking, solution to whatever problem you may have. Idly think of the pros and cons and note them. This clears your subconscious and unconscious mind.

You may wish to question your dreaming mind about health, in which case you may want to ask questions such as 'How can I heal myself?', 'What am I meant to learn through this illness?' 'How can I handle pain?', 'How can I handle the reaction of those around me?', 'How can I deal with the fear of death?', 'How can I keep my body in an optimum state of health?'

If you have a problem, a decision to make or a relationship question, follow the same principle. Write down your own perception of the problem, your question and the possible solution (from a detached point of view) to get it out of the way.

With practice, you can mentally incubate dreams but I personally find the result is better when I write down and sleep on what I have written.

Finally (although none of this preparation needs to take hours of time), lie on your bed or relax in a chair and visualize entering the temples of Delphi or Epidaurus, as they were in the past. Let your imagination run free, but if you have any difficulties, you may find it helpful to look at pictures of ancient Greek temples. Imagine being greeted by priests who lead you to comfortable couches or mats on the floor. Know that as you drift into sleep, your questions will be answered.

You may prefer to visualize entering the ancient city of Petra, in Jordan, where healers lived in caves with their patients until they were cured or died, or to imagine Atlantean healing, in which people bathed in herbal waters and were flooded with light and vibration from crystals or colour before entering an inner healing sanctum.

Another visualization, which I have found very powerful, is the one designed by Paul Solomon in which one imagines climbing (easily!) a mountain consisting of many coloured gardens. These gardens follow the colour spectrum of red to violet and end with white light or white cloud at the top, where there is a temple, hut or cave, whatever appears or feels correct in one's imagination. At this point, imagine entering the place with a gift, presenting it and lying down to sleep.

Alternatively, imagine finding a library or being given your book of life which will give you the answers your need. These exercises can also be used to contact your own guardian angel, spiritual helpers or higher soul consciousness.

When you awake, write down any thoughts and ideas you might have as the result of your dream or visualization experience. Remember, too, that your answers may come or be added to by overhearing a conversation on a train, reading a newspaper article or watching a television programme. Notice everything that happens in the course of your day and watch and listen to the signs and signals, the hints and nudges that the universe constantly gives us and which most of us usually ignore. If after a few days, you need greater clarity, write down 'I need greater clarity or deeper understanding' – or whatever, even if it's a repeat of the dream, and sleep with the paper under your pillow. If you have never paid attention to your dreams before, you need to let your dreaming mind know that you are now seriously ready to listen.

Similar preparation, leaving out the visualization exercises, can be used for your own personal vision quest. If you have the time and a suitable place, a vision quest is best done outside, even in your own garden if you can be alone and undisturbed. You *do* need to be alone for this. To create a sacred space, collect bits and pieces from the countryside around you that for some reason have an impact on you – birds' feathers, small stones, a piece of wood or branch, flowers, berries, leaves etc. Do *not* pick up anything that does not strike a responsive chord on some level. When you have gathered enough objects, make a circle with them, big enough to sit in. If you decide to make a two- or three-day event of this with a tent, arrange your objects around the tent. If you are only going to do it for a day or an hour or two, arrange your circle in as comfortable a place as possible. If you need to lean against something, make your circle around a tree and use its trunk for support. Alternatively, you could draw a circle in the earth or sand and place your objects in and around it in the same way.

You are, in a sense, creating a simple form of Medicine Wheel and you will add to its power by acknowledging the North, South, East and West. This can be done by placing the element associated with each one in place. For example, the element for the North is air, and you could use a picture of a hurricane or trees blowing in the breeze; the element for the South is water, and you could place a small bottle or glass of water there; the element for the West is earth and you could use soil or something from the mineral kingdom; the element for the East is fire, so a candle, a box of matches, a picture of a fire, or the sun could serve as its symbol.

Take the time to face each direction in turn and ask for its powers to assist you. For example, you might ask the wind to blow away your past and clear your mind, the water to heal your emotions, the earth to support you physically, and the fire to inspire and renew your spirit.

If you do not have a garden, do exactly the same at home in your bedroom or sitting-room. If you are sick, disabled or bedbound, do the same exercises in your imagination.

When you are ready to sit or lie inside your circle, take time to focus on where you are in your life. What are your achievements, failures, talents, weak points, fears and joys? Are your relationships happy and if not, why not? Are you fulfilled, energetic and full of life, or tired, bored and depressed? What do you need to change in yourself or your life? Have you faced and integrated your Shadow – that part of ourselves that we repress or do not like?

When you have thought about your life and the answers or guidance you seek, close your eyes, relax and breathe in through your nose to the count of four, hold the breath to the count of four and sigh the breath out to the count of four until you feel slightly spacey and relaxed. Ask for an animal to be shown to you, one whose strength and energy you can draw on throughout your life. This might come as an image or a word; it might be wild or tame – even the family cat. Whatever comes, imagine questioning it … Why this particular animal? What are its qualities? How can it help you? What does it want you to know? If it is an animal you fear, go into the fear and ask why it has come. Imagine saying, 'I need help, guidance and support for the next phase of my life/to recover from this illness/divorce/loss of job/for greater knowledge/spiritual enlightenment' – whatever you need help for. Try and do this on an empty stomach and without a drink beside you. If your stomach is trying to

digest food, it will detract and distract you from what can be a profound experience.

Record the feelings and thoughts that come during and after the experience and if you decide to do this regularly, note the changes that occur in yourself and your life on both inner and outer levels.

Of course this is not a 'proper' vision quest or Medicine Wheel, but it can lead to a sense of connection to a source of knowledge and energy that can empower you to live your life in a courageous and fulfilling way. Too many of us reach a point of loss, change or emptiness where we question the meaning and purpose of life and, instead of literally going to the woods or mountains, instead of using these times as an opportunity to delve into our innermost being, we rush out and buy new cars, or clothes, change our partners, dye our hair, get into drugs and alcohol, or do anything else that suppresses the inner voice that is trying so hard to communicate.

A circle, no matter whether it is physically created, drawn or imagined, can have an extremely powerful effect. While living in Australia, I began to draw huge circles – or, as Jung described them, mandalas – and filled them with the colours and symbols that appeared in meditation. At night, as I went to sleep, I felt myself sucked into the middle of what I had drawn that day. My dreams were extraordinary and during that year, my whole life changed.

The circle is probably the most ancient and meaningful symbol of all time – rock carvings world-wide, historical sites such as Stonehenge, the Maze in Chartres cathedral, Tibetan and Indian mandalas, sand paintings and Medicine Wheels are all based on it.

Black Elk, an elder of the Dakota tribe, once said, 'Everything the Power of the World does, is done in a circle,' and Kenneth Meadows, author of *The Medicine Way*, defines the Medicine Wheel as 'a circle of knowledge that restores wholeness and gives power over one's life'.

Try it and see for yourself.

HOW TO STIMULATE DREAMING

'I am sure that there are some simple secrets, some methods that can be learned, means of which we may in some measure command our dreams, and that more than we yet realise the control of our dreams lies in our power.'

MARY ARNOLD FOSTER, STUDIES OF DREAMS

Everybody dreams but not everyone remembers their dreams. This may be because most of us grew up with the belief that dreams were unimportant, a meaningless jumble of mental garbage, or fragments, left over from the day's events and irrelevant to our waking lives. But in order to use our dreams to enhance our lives, we must first be able to remember what they are!

Dream research has shown that we all dream four or five times a night and that during REM sleep, certain brain cells turn on while others turn off. The cells that turn off release neurotransmitters, chemicals that are crucial to attention, learning and memory – this may be another reason why so many of us forget our dreams. As already mentioned REM sleep begins about 90 minutes after we fall asleep. At the same time the brain speeds up, blood pressure rises, breathing quickens and the heart beats faster. Despite the fact that our muscles relax, we may twitch, or even mutter and sigh under our breath. We are in another world, a self-created universe. Episodes of REM dreams, which occur every 90 minutes, are separated by periods of calmer, deeper, non-REM or slow-wave sleep. Non-REM shows brain activity, but statistically less dreaming. We spend approximately two hours, or 25 per cent, of each night in REM, which, as we have seen, adds up to six years in an average lifetime.

A sleep laboratory study of language students showed that students who had more REM or dream sleep were those who learned the fastest. In her book *Breakthrough Dreaming* Dr Gayle Delaney says that:

> 'These studies suggest that dreaming plays an important role in processing new information even when we recall no dreams. Although our forgotten dreams probably give us new ideas and insights far more frequently than we suspect, bringing our dreams into conscious awareness will greatly enhance their usefulness.'

This has certainly been proven time and again. Otto Loewi, for example, a research pharmacologist at New York College of Medicine, wanted to know if nerves sent signals by transmitting electricity or by a chemical signal. He dreamed the answer and in laboratory tests it worked. He won a Nobel prize. In a dream, the scientist Niels Bohr saw the structure of the atom, which led to his work in atomic physics and atomic energy. Edison and Einstein both used dreamlike states to solve problems. Einstein gazed at clouds drifting in the sky until he felt his mind swimming. Edison used to fast and keep himself awake for two or three days. He then sat with a ball-bearing in each hand, so that when he began to fall asleep, they would drop to the floor with a resounding thud and wake him. Light-headed

from lack of food and sleep, like Einstein in a semi-altered state of consciousness, he knew this was the moment to ask questions and get answers to problems his waking mind found insoluble. Claude Lelouche, the film-director, said, 'People don't realize that dreams are the most determinant element in our lives. I dream a film before I make it. Someone had to dream the place or TV before they were invented.' Many of my own workshop ideas have come from my dreams so I know that we do not have to have creative or intellectual genius to use dreams to solve problems and inspire new thoughts.

The power to control, stimulate and remember our dreams begins with the simple step of deciding to value them. If we were to do no more than impress upon our unconscious, subconscious and higher conscious minds that we are really serious about dreams, and respect and honour the information they contain, the quality of our dreaming would automatically improve.

If you have never paid attention to your dreams before, it may take one or two weeks of practice to obtain results, but if you use some of the following suggestions you will not only dream but also remember your dreams. In fact, many people have almost instant dream recall after reading one or two dream books. This is an excellent way to begin to set in motion your dreaming mind's co-operation.

The initial preparation for vivid and memorable dreams is virtually the same as for a sound night's sleep (see pages 18–32). However, a brief recap is as follows:

1. Create a peaceful atmosphere in your bedroom using bright or soothing colours, flowers, crystals, candles, music, light, incense, herbs, pictures, plants and anything else that makes you feel relaxed and happy.
2. Move your bed North, South, West or East and see which position gives you the best dreams. It is said that the

bedhead placed North gives the best results, but it is more important to discover what suits you.

3. Remember that pillows filled with herbs can induce both sleep and dreams. A dream pillow should be made of cotton or silk, fairly flat and not more than 15 by 12" (38 by 31 cm). Among many recipes, one that is highly effective mixes together one part rosemary, lavender and sweet marjoram and half a part of thyme and spearmint. Then add one tablespoon of orris root powder, one tablespoon of dried orange peel and one teaspoon of powdered cinnamon. Mix well and put in the bag, which must be placed under the pillow and slightly to one side so that the warmth from the sleeper's head causes the herbs to exude their fragrance and induce a sound natural sleep and inspirational dreams.

   A recipe for a dream-promoting herbal tisane uses half a tablespoon of fresh or dried rosemary, mixed with one and a quarter cups of cold water, brought to the boil and sweetened with honey.
4. Leave the day behind. Briefly sum it up and write it down. This will also help dream interpretation. If you hate writing, mentally sum up the day and breathe the memory of it into a crystal or let it float away in a bath or a shower or by soaking your feet in warm water. If you shower, imagine standing in the rain or under a waterfall – if you can literally do this, even better. (N.B. if you use the ginger bath recipe (see page 91), do *not* do it every night – it is a powerful treatment and should only be used occasionally.)
5. Relaxation is a key element in sleep and dream preparation, and among the most important methods is control of your breathing. In addition to the other breathing exercises I have described, the following technique, which

stimulates both dreams and relaxation, is probably the most powerful:

a) Kneel back on your haunches, with both hands resting, palms up, on your knees.

b) Close your eyes, inhale to the count of six, hold the breath in to the count of six and then exhale to the count of six. Do this sequence at least six times each for maximum benefit, although it can be done as many times as you like.

c) With your eyes still closed, touch the tip of the little finger to the top of the thumb on each hand. Continue the same rhythm of breathing.

d) Extend the little fingers and thumbs, while folding the three middle fingers of each hand into the palms, continue the in, down and out to count of six breathing.

e) Close all the fingers over the thumb on each hand, making a fist. Continue to breathe as before.

f) Go back to step a) and open your hands, palms up and continue the in, down and out to count of six breathing. Gradually relax into normal breathing.

This exercise not only stimulates dreams, but can also be used by people who are sleepless or in great pain. If it is too uncomfortable to kneel, sit in a chair. If you are in bed, lie on your back with your arms resting alongside your body and your hands open, palms upwards. As you practise this, you will notice that the movements of the fingers alter where the air goes in the lungs. Even people who swear they never remember dreams have had almost immediate success after this exercise.

6. Crystals are excellent catalysts both for dreaming and remembering your dreams. Put them under the pillow, on a bedside table, on the floor, in the bed or around it. I have a double-terminated (pointed at both ends) crystal that is

like my closest, dearest, very best friend. We travel, work and sleep together. However, very occasionally I find that with this crystal under my pillow I cannot sleep and have to remove it to another room.

If you decide to use crystals to stimulate dreams, remember that the clearer and more sparkling a crystal is, the more energizing it will be. The more opaque it, or any other gem, is, the more soothing and calming its effect.

Amethyst, rose quartz and blue lace agate are good 'sleep-inducers'. Amethyst, in particular, if you are stressed, will absorb and transmute emotional trauma. Moonstone and selenite, two gems associated with the moon, contain within them the moon's power to give visions. Sugilite, so named after its discovery by Japanese Professor Sugi, and sometimes called luvalite, activates intuition, imagination and the dreaming side of the brain. Rutilated quartz (a crystal with fine silver, gold or grey threads running through it like miniature telephone wires) helps connect past, present and future, as do dreams, and can also connect us to other realities.

Any of these gems can be placed in water and left outside to absorb the moon's rays overnight. To drink moon-energized water before sleep is a delightful way to enhance dreaming.

7. Another good preparation for dreams is to attune to and then balance the chakras. These are seven vital centres placed at intervals between the top of the head and the sacrum at the base of the spine. They are like power points where lines of energy meet and cross. *Chakra* in Sanskrit means 'wheel' and each chakra, when healthy, is a whirling vortex or wheel of energy.

The main chakras are the root, spleen or sacral, solar plexus, heart, throat, brow or third eye and crown. The root or base chakra is connected to the base of the spine and has to do with survival, reproduction/sexuality and all aspects of earthly life. The spleen chakra is just below the navel and is the area where we feel 'gut-level' emotion, which can either empower or block creativity and expression. The solar plexus is at the diaphragm and is associated with communication, relationships, social identity and self-esteem. The heart chakra is at heart or thymus level. It is the chakra of unconditional love and acceptance of ourselves and others, as well as our link between the lower and higher chakras, Heaven and Earth, the visible and invisible. The throat chakra is at the throat and, like the solar plexus, is associated with communication, but more in the sense of expressing our own truth, will and identity than in social contact with others. The third eye or brow chakra is at the centre of the forehead, between and slightly above the eyebrows. It is the seat of intuition, imagination and spiritual insight. The crown chakra is located at the top of the head and is a level of spiritual understanding, spiritual opening, a doorway of communication with angels, guides and our own divinity.

There are many ways to assess the balance or imbalance of our chakras and it is a good thing to do from time to time, because the flow of energy between the chakras affects not only our dreams but also our physical health and sense of well-being:

a) We can read chakra books and see which classification strikes a chord in us.
b) We can use a pendulum, or rather get a friend to do so, to check them out.
c) We can use imagination/visualization by mentally focusing on each chakra and seeing or sensing the colours or symbols that pop up.

d) We can use Kinesiology or Touch for Health, which is also an excellent (though not always 100 per cent accurate) technique for allergy testing. For this, first extend your left arm and let someone press down on your wrist while you 'resist', or hold your arm straight. Do *not* fight for control – simply allow the person to feel your normal muscle strength. Then place your right hand on each chakra in turn and again extend your left arm to be pressed. If the chakra is weak, your arm will drop slightly; if strong, your arm will lift up a little. (N.B. Relax your left arm and body between each chakra by shaking yourself and dropping your arm to your side.)

e) I sometimes check my own chakras by hand scanning, although it is better to get someone else to do this. Simply shake your hands vigorously to recharge their electromagnetic field and then hold them, right hand above left, palms facing the body, a few inches above each chakra. With practice, you will sense a difference if one is not as active as another.

If you find your chakras are out of synch, one simple exercise to clear and balance them is to hold a crystal, point down, or facing towards each chakra, and rotate it for a few moments, a few inches above or away from each one. This is similar to the hand-sensing, except you are now directing energy into the chakras. To do this, follow the natural clockwise or anti-clockwise movement of each chakra. In a woman, the chakra is anti-clockwise at the crown, clockwise at the brow, anti-clockwise at the throat, clockwise at the heart, anti-clockwise at the solar plexus, clockwise at the spleen and anti-clockwise at the root or base chakra. For a man it is the exact opposite: clockwise at the crown, anti-clockwise at the brow and so forth. If you make an anti-clockwise movement on a chakra whose natural flow is clockwise, it is a little like suddenly scraping a scab on a wound and can cause discomfort.

Another exercise involves the use of colour and/or light, either by visualizing specific colours, or light, filling each chakra (see below), or by placing coloured stones, tiny pieces of fabric or embroidery threads on them. I learned to do this from indigenous healers in Sri Lanka. I find it more powerful if I chant sounds that correspond to each colour. The sounds I use are ones I learned from William David, an extraordinary spiritual teacher and ex-opera singer.

Each chakra is associated with a particular colour and to correlate the colours and sounds with the relevant chakras is a wonderful pre-sleep and dream, as well as pre-meditation, exercise. The colours and sounds are as follows:

Colour	**Sound**	**Pitch**	**Chakra**
red	ee	C	base
orange	eh	G	spleen/sacral
yellow	aah	E	solar plexus
green	ay	D	heart
blue	oh	B	throat
indigo	om	F	third eye/brow
violet	oo	A	crown
white	I am	any pitch	Beyond all chakras and meaning 'I am one with the Source of Life, the heart, the body, the mind of god.'

8. Make sure you have everything that you need to record your dreams – a pen, pencil, notepad or journal, or a tape-recorder, and a torch – beside your bed before you go to sleep. If you awake with a dream in your head you should record it at once. If you have to search for paper and pen, the dream is likely to vanish. Although a tape-recorder is often easier to use, writing down a dream impresses it more deeply on the consciousness and is a further signal to your dreaming mind that you are seriously paying attention. It is helpful to keep an Ephemeris (an astrological table or calendar) beside the bed, too, to check the zodiac signs through which the moon is passing, because the moon's phases affect our dreams.
9. Before turning out the light do not forget to write down 'I want to dream and I want to remember my dreams.' Remember that to ask a dream for help, healing or insight is a form of dream incubation and it will work better if you immerse yourself in the subject of your question, as well as concentrate on it before sleep. Once the light is out, mentally repeat, 'I am going to dream and remember my dreams.' If you want to fly or astral travel in your dreams, remember the flight of birds and imagine you too can lift up and fly away.
10. An effective dream trigger is to put a glass of water next to the bed and drink half of it just before sleep, affirming 'I *will* dream. I *will* remember my dreams.' Immediately you awake, drink the other half and repeat the affirmation. This helps to fix the idea of dreaming in your mental computer. If you do this, you can add a small crystal to your water for even greater effect. Another trigger is to set an alarm to wake you every one and a half hours

and immediately write down any dream you remember. If you remember nothing, note the first thoughts that come into your mind. Although this course of action is somewhat drastic and may be unpopular if you have a 'non-interested-in-dreams' sleeping partner, it works within two or three days and is usually needed only once.

11. Vitamin B_6 and niacin can be helpful for both dreaming and dream recall. A shortage of B_6 – the 'mental vitamin' – makes it difficult to remember dreams and all the B vitamins help counteract stress and emotional imbalance.
12. As you lie down to sleep you are moving from day, or personality school, to night, or soul school for spiritual instruction. To have a sense of reverence, to attune to your own higher soul self, angels, guides and teachers, clears the way for a different level of information to come through your dreams. This can be done through prayer, meditation, chanting, by repeating a mantra, or singing the *Om*. The prayer or mantra can be in your own words and could include asking for protection and guidance while asleep. Even to say no more than 'I am going to sleep and dream to get in touch with the highest within me' is enough to direct your conscious self to soul-level wisdom.
13. Yet another way to stimulate empowering dreams is to practise 20–30 minutes' meditation twice a day. This can provide as much benefit as three or four hours' sleep.
14. Pre-sleep visualization exercises can also induce deep sleep and more profound dreams. In fact if you believe you do not dream or dream only rarely, you might want to visualize yourself dreaming, remembering the dream and waking to write it down. You could also imagine speaking to a specific dream teacher or guide and ask for help in both having and remembering dreams. You

might dedicate a particular T-shirt to dreams and wear it when you want a specific dream. You could imagine going to visit a house of dreams, a boat of dreams, a field of dreams – anything that inspires your imagination. To hang a Native American dream-catcher net above or near your bed can also inspire wonderful dreams. The main point to remember is that all visualization techniques slow the brainwave rhythm from beta to alpha and help pre-sleep relaxation. The more creative you are before sleep, the more colourful and enjoyable your dreams are likely to be.

Do not be put off by this list – it may look daunting, but all the techniques are simple and effective, and none of them take a lot of time. Pick whichever of these ideas feel right for you, and adapt or develop them to your own needs. You will probably find that one or two work better for you than others. Remember, too, that most of us dream – or remember our dreams – *less* when tired, overworked or emotionally stressed. Sleeping pills, drugs and alcohol can also interfere with our ability to dream.

To invoke, pay attention to and use the wisdom of dreams in one's daily life is a profound spiritual discipline. However, it also needs to be fun. Do not take it so seriously that you cloud the internal magic mirror on which dreams are revealed. Expect to sleep and dream with joy, pleasure and delight – and you will.

HOW TO EXPLORE AND USE DREAMS

> If one advances confidently in the direction of his dreams, and endeavours to use the life which he has imagined, he will meet with a success unexpected in common hours.
>
> HENRY DAVID THOREAU

Marie Louise von Franz, a colleague of Jung's, once said, 'The dream is always unique, always comes at the right moment. It is a message from the powers of the instinct, the powers of the collective unconscious, a message which comes during a particular night, which is meant specifically for the dreamer.' To Jung, as already mentioned, the collective unconscious contained the wisdom of the ages. He believed that the more attuned to it man was, through dreams, visions and active imagination, the more balanced, integrated and happy his life and personality would be. He thought that dreams were notably a vital part of the psyche's balancing system but also a means of coming to terms with the whole of life. He also believed that the unconscious offered guidance unobtainable from any other source and he found that many of his mid-life crisis patients who described feelings of isolation and emptiness were really suffering from separation from the rich, emotional life of the unconscious.

Long before this, the Roman soothsayer Artemidorous of Ephesus wrote a book on dreams which had a profound effect on all subsequent dream research. Artemidorous drew on both the Egyptian and Greek civilizations for the material for his book the *Oneirocritica*, and, like them suggested that 'Dreams and visions are infused into men for their advantage and instruction.' Hundreds of years later, Edgar Cayce said, 'All dreams are given for the benefit of the dreamer – would that he interpret them correctly.' Unfortunately, most of us struggle through life just trying to cope, without making any attempt to use our dreams to contact this almost immortal source of wisdom, inspiration, balance and healing that could transform our lives.

Yet dreams honestly reflect what we feel and think about ourselves and life – they are, in the words of Calvin Hall, a psychologist and dream researcher, 'pictures of the mind'. So, if we can get meaning from a picture we can get meaning from a dream.

EXPLORING DREAMS

Out of dozens of methods of exploring and integrating dreams into our daily lives the ones I describe in this chapter are those which I have myself successfully used over many years. They work as well with groups as with individuals, and many of them are also suitable for and popular with children.

One of my favourite ways to both record and explore a dream consists of the following eight very simple steps:

1. Give the dream a title which embodies its essence and which will, on re-reading it, weeks, months or years later, immediately remind you of its story.

2. Describe the main action – such as running away, typing a letter, acting in a play, driving a car… Are these activities common or peculiar to your daily life? If so, why?
3. Note the feelings in the dream, plus, later, your waking feelings about the dream, and how these relate to your daily life, i.e. do you experience the same emotions awake or asleep?
4. Outline the dream setting – is it natural or man-made? A natural setting is one in which forests, mountains, lakes, beaches, parks and gardens appear, while man-made settings include cars, trains, buses, city streets, airports, buildings, computers etc. Does the setting change from one category to the other?
5. Describe the people, their qualities, plus what part of you or who in your life they remind you of.
6. List the symbols and objects – especially those that in some way stand out.
7. Sum up in as few words as possible what the dream appears to be saying. (Do this spontaneously, intuitively, and without reference to an 'official' dream interpretation book.)
8. Actualize the dream by performing in your waking life the action suggested by the dream's message.

To record a dream in this way captures the key points without having to write out the whole story. If you have no time to do more than write, for example:

Title	White Parrot
Action	Running, dancing.
Feelings	Laughter – freedom – anxiety.
Setting	Dance-hall.
People	Boss – next-door neighbour – guard on train.
Symbols	Parrot – train – shoe – dancers.

you can later sum up what each aspect of the dream means to you, together with its message.

Our 'White Parrot' dreamer said that for her the parrot (as the title) meant love and chatter; the action of running and dancing combined freedom, performance and release; the feeling of laughter and freedom was the past, while anxiety meant stress; the dance-hall was excitement; the boss, authority, the neighbour, a friend, the guard, protection and security; the dancers were companions. The main symbols of parrot, train, shoe and dancers signified communication, journey, walking and freedom. The message for her was to release old memories, face her fear of authority, which was causing her stress, and walk into a new life of love and companionship, knowing she was protected, guarded and guided all the way. When I asked her what her main sense of the message was she looked me straight in the eye and said, 'Freedom.' This dreamer was a person who, although full of fun and humour, had been bullied by father, step-father and husband. Her dream actualization could have been a) to walk away from a stressful situation; b) to take small steps to assert her independence by making time for friends and to relax and have fun. She chose the latter solution – and, despite her husband's disapproval, also bought two lovebirds! Her life is now much happier.

Symbols have different meanings for different people, of course.

George, using the same symbols, came up with 'caged' for White Parrot, 'movement' and 'impossible' for the running and dancing; 'joy, holiday and overwork' for the laughter, freedom and anxiety; 'entertainment' for the dance-hall; the boss was 'stifling', the neighbour 'helpful', the guard meant 'tickets', the dancers were 'exuberance'. The parrot, train, shoes and dancers symbolized 'poor bird, travel, steps and freedom'. He summed this up to mean (for him): 'Stop feeling overworked and hemmed in – take steps, or get a move on, to organize tickets for

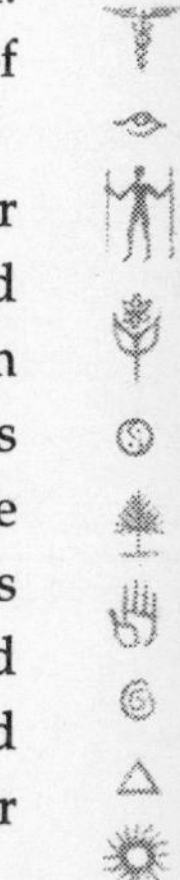

an exciting holiday! Action a) call the nearest travel agent or air line and book tickets or b) acquire a few travel brochures or c) take mini vacations and explore the local area during weekends.' When George briefly summed up the dream's message he simply said, 'Trapped and overworked.' But, no matter what action he takes to respond to this, even the most minimal response of, for example, sitting on a park bench for half an hour at lunch-time, his dreaming self will, in turn, act on his response and give him more energy to cope.

This is a basic and simple way to record and work with a dream. As you become more proficient, you may want to write down every detail of a dream and explore every minute facet of it.

A similar method, developed by Dr Gayle Delaney and Dr Lorna Flowers at their dream centre in America, is to:

1. Place a rectangle around each setting in a dream.
2. Circle each person.
3. Underline each animal and major object.
4. Circle each feeling with a wavy cloud.
5. Underline with an arrow the major actions.

This highlights the major elements of the dream, which can then elicit the dreamer's own descriptions and associations.

Many of us ignore the dream setting as irrelevant to the main dream story. However, the setting is similar to the backdrop of a theatre stage – it helps set the scene and gives clues for whatever subsequently takes place. According to Jung, 'The description of the locality is very important; the place where the dream is staged, whether hotel, station, street, wood, under water, etc., makes a tremendous difference in the interpretation.'

I have found that, generally speaking, dreams whose settings fall into the category of 'man-made', such as vehicles, streets, buildings, and so forth, are to do with the personality, while those with background settings of woods and meadows, flowers, lakes and rivers are direct communication with the soul or inner self. (Of course all dreams are ultimately soul-oriented, but this defines which aspect is the target of the dream story.) A change of setting indicates a shift of feeling or focus.

Feelings are the most important feature of every dream. We should include in our dream analysis – though not necessarily at the moment of writing the dream down – not only how we feel *within* the dream but also how we feel *awake*, about the setting, the people, the events, the actions we make or observe, the objects and symbols that may pop up.

Dreams pluck from our innermost parts feelings which most of us have learned to suppress, to the point where we do not even know what our true feelings are, and present them to us disguised as pictures, symbols and metaphors. When we translate the images back into feelings we can recognize, we can come to terms with our true emotions, which in turn can lead to a dramatic healing of the psyche, especially in the areas of love, forgiveness, trust and compassion, for both ourselves and others.

Mark, a highly successful and somewhat arrogant businessman, dreamed of a man encased in steel-plated armour that threatened to stifle him to death. Mark released the headpiece to find he was face to face with himself. Shocked, he awoke and realized that from the age of eight, when his mother had abandoned him, he had armoured himself against his feelings in order to survive.

Tom had grown up in a family of women who treated him like a toy puppy. If he played on the street with friends, came home dirty, refused to eat all the foot on his plate or listened to loud music in his bedroom when he was meant to be asleep, the women cried. He learned that if he was to survive in the world, and avoid trouble, especially around women, he must placate both them and the world. When he was around 40 years old, he dreamed of toy dogs suddenly becoming alive. To his astonishment stuffed poodles began to growl, bark, show their teeth and wag their tails. Miniature toy terriers developed lions' manes, grew in size and roared. These dreams put Tom in touch with his own, totally unconscious, survival strategies and helped him to move beyond them.

Gay had recurring dreams in which she watched a man being stabbed to death by a hand that wore an unusual iron bracelet. She felt overwhelmed with sadness but did nothing to help prevent the death. Later she suddenly remembered that as a very young child, two or three years old, she had seen an almost identical bracelet on her grandmother's wrist. After her grandmother's death, the bracelet had been worn by Gay's mother. Gay had always wanted to be a doctor, but after listening to constant statements from both mother and grandmother along the lines of 'Medicine is a career for men', 'Only men should go to university/study/travel/train for a specific job…', 'Girls do not need qualifications', 'Girls get married', 'It's not feminine to want a full-time career', 'Girls must have babies', she stifled her ambitions. The dream showed her that she had allowed the iron grip of her grandmother's ideas, subsequently inherited by her mother, to kill her initiative, her masculine energy and her 'get up and go' in order to conform to their expectations. Although saddened by her realization, Gay, at 52, said to herself, 'Better late than never' and embarked on a career as a hospice worker.

Before these dreams, neither Mark nor Tom nor Gay were aware of how they had stifled themselves and their feelings to cope with the world around them. They finally realized that they had continued doing to themselves what others had done and said to them. They also saw that they were perpetuating the same negative messages to their own families and were unconsciously inviting others to treat them in the same negative way.

(N.B. Even our body language and tone of voice reveal to others how we expect to be treated. Ted, a financial whizz kid, operating with other people's money, said that when introduced to people with limp, 'wet-fish' handshakes, he knew he could manipulate them. When the handshake was firm and strong, he had to be on his toes.)

All of us, of course, consciously and unconsciously develop ways to cope with life from childhood onwards. Survival techniques include temper tantrums, bullying, refusal to listen, silence, withdrawal, possessiveness, frigidity, stubborness, self-pity, depression, illness, self-denial, self-depreciation, over-anxiety to please others, placating, perfectionism, caustic remarks that put people down, sexual teasing, resistance to authority, clowning, and irritability, as well as constant criticism and disapproval of everything from the Royal Family to the latest fashions and the teenagers next door. For many of us these patterns become so deeply embedded that we are unconscious of them until our dreams and/or our friends point them out. But to live our lives using behavioural techniques based on survival from childhood means we perpetuate the idea of ourselves as victims. If we felt, as the French say *bien dans nos peaux* (well, or comfortable, in our skins), we would not need to do any of these things. We would accept ourselves and the world around us as it is. Dreams can help us to do this.

One of the first steps to heal victim consciousness is to find the lost child most of us have buried inside us, the 'inner child' needs as much love and care as any physical child. We can use dreams and visualization to get in touch with this part of ourselves. With love, attention, reassurance and understanding, the child will then co-operate with, rather than fight against, us.

Most of learn in childhood that we get more attention when we are naughty and difficult than when we are obedient, good and nice. In the same way if we neglect our inner children, they, too, will behave badly – in the form of creating mood swings, lack of confidence and anything else that can disturb our happiness – in order to get our attention.

A dream that shocked me into realizing how badly I treated my own inner child came in response to a specific question that I wrote down before sleep in which I asked for help in getting in touch with it. When I saw the starving, swollen-bellied, dirty, bruised, runny-nosed, miserable little creature that appeared as a result, I was appalled – even more so when a nursemaid appeared and said firmly, '*This* is *your* baby.' The shock and pain that exploded inside me with her words woke me up. I realized I was neglecting myself and the baby as much as I had been neglected in childhood. The dream forced me to review my life and see how I could heal the baby by changing the way I treated myself. I also used waking-life visualization, or Active Imagination as it is sometimes called, to clean, cradle, feed and comfort the baby. I had to do this many times before its little stick-like arms began to get a little fatter.

Another way to invoke a dream in which you can see and communicate with an abandoned or lost part of yourself is to ask yourself, as you turn out the light, 'How old is the child in me *now*, at this moment?' A number will pop up – one day it may be three, another day eight, nine, ten or five. As you drift into sleep, mentally review your life at that age and ask for a dream to give you insight into what that child might need now to be healed, whole and happy. Immediately you wake, write down what you think the child may need – even if you do not remember a specific dream. Then visualize, either immediately, or when it is convenient, giving the child what it needs.

A friend who did this found an eight-year-old boy staggering under a pile of bricks that were loaded onto his shoulders. Awake, with closed eyes, he asked the child what the bricks meant. 'Responsibilities,' the boy replied. Suddenly Duncan remembered that when he was eight his father had left home. His mother, heavily pregnant, had begun to use Duncan as a substitute husband in the sense of getting him to shop, generally fetch and carry, and keep the house and garden tidy until her baby was born. Unfortunately it was a difficult birth and mother and baby took months to recover. Duncan became the man of the house and this, combined with his schoolwork, left him no time for fun and play. He grew into a nice, hard-working over-responsible man who never let anyone else help him. Duncan visualized saying to his long-forgotten eight-year-old self, 'I am so very sorry that I left you here to carry this load alone. You do not need to do so any longer. I am going to take it away immediately.' He removed the bricks one by one until the boy stood straight and free and then took him in his arms and hugged him so hard he felt as if they merged together. After Duncan had done this he wept for a long time but his shoulders relaxed and his body felt light. From time to time before sleep, Duncan invokes dreams in which he and the boy can play, have fun and explore the world. He is much more relaxed about life now.

If you have negative feelings that literally thwart or control your life, make a list of the most commonly experienced ones and note how they affect you, the situations in which they are most likely to arise and what happens if you express them. Take one emotion at a time and before sleep close your eyes and imagine a symbol for it. When it is reasonably clear in your mind's eye, mentally say, 'How old was I when I first experienced the emotion?' Let the number pop up spontaneously, and again remember yourself at that age, while at the same time asking for a dream that will deepen your understanding. Hold the image of the symbol as you drift into sleep. Immediately you awake, note any thoughts and feelings that come to you. Just as Duncan did, hug, hold and reassure the child you were

at the age of the number that came up – even if you do not remember literally dreaming of them. This is a simple and effective way to heal wounded parts of ourselves.

You can also imagine talking to this child or person and asking what they need or want from you. Then give whatever it may be – and some hugs and love too. You might add words to the effect of 'I want to get to know you better, share with you what makes me happy and unhappy, what I like and do not like doing, and I want you to feel free to share the same things with me ...'

When you have completed the exercise re-visualize the emotion symbol and check for any changes. If it is no longer exactly the same, it shows that a part of you is beginning to heal. If there is no change, do not despair, simply remember that most healing requires more than one dose of a particular medicine or remedy.

This is a wonderful and simple way to discover and heal the source of some of our wounded parts which can then lead to major transformation.

Dream actions, and especially what we feel about them, as we either observe or carry them out, are another indication of what the overall dream theme is trying to communicate. If a dream is so action-packed that there is no time to record every event, we should pick the one or two most bizarre or striking activities and drop the rest.

Always look at how dream activities relate to, or contradict, anything in waking life. Gayle Delaney has a wonderful system of dream interviewing in which she suggests we question every facet of a dream from the perspective of a newly arrived alien from another planet:

> 'When you find the action of a dream to be rather prosaic and uninteresting, make your curiosity burn. Remind yourself that this may be an important clue to the meaning of the dream, and

for all you know could be described by an alien in unpredictable and unexpected terms.'

Dream escapades encompass everything from strolling along a beach or street with a friend to flying to the moon on angels' wings or cavorting as a clown in a circus ring. From the sublime to the ridiculous, they all clue us in to a dream's overall meaning. Amongst the enormous range of activities we get up to in dreams – which can include anything we might have seen, heard of or done in waking life – some of the most common are the following: being chased; running away; falling off cliffs or out of windows, down stairwells, into black holes or dark pools of water; getting stuck in narrow tunnels or airless caves; searching for toilets; urinating or defecating in public places, driving cars, or any other form of transport; flying; running to catch trains, planes or buses; dancing on stage or presenting a public lecture and suddenly realizing you are either semi-naked or completely so; searching for handbags, wallets, money, tickets and passports; trying to find a way out of a maze of rooms or looking for specific people down corridors that never end. All these dreams are very common.

We need to look at how comfortable we felt both during and after the dream. Do running, falling or flying give you a sense of exhilaration or panic? Do you feel anxious, vulnerable or quite happy to search for a toilet and then sit on it in the middle of a busy store or restaurant? If you are involved with a vehicle, are you confident or nervous in the driver's seat, or are you stuck behind or in front of it pushing or pulling? If you find yourself naked in front of a crowd of people are you embarrassed or indifferent – and do they notice? If you are searching for a passport, money or hidden jewels, are you excited and expectant or fearful of not finding what you seek? If you are running, are you running away from or towards a person or situation?

No matter what our dream activities may be, they mirror what we do in waking life. For instance, if you run away in dreams, is there something in life you avoid – something you cannot, or will not, face? Flying dreams usually signify expansion and access to higher and greater abilities, as well as astral travel and lucid dreaming, but if you fly continually, it can imply not having your feet on the ground, living in a fantasy world and refusing to deal with everyday realities. To search for lost passports, ID cards, licences, wallets and purses, hidden diaries, keys and treasure suggests we are looking for lost, 'put to one side' buried parts of ourselves, as well as for old identities which we need to replace with new ones. In both waking and dreaming life, when facing major turning-points, I have lost my passport – or had it stolen – and have had to get a new one. Another perfect candidate for passport dreams would be a woman whose children finally leave home to establish independent lives and who feels a loss of identity as a mother and a need to find or create a new role for herself.

Dreams of being naked or semi-naked and toilet-type dreams *can* symbolize a healthy willingness to expose ourselves, to happily reveal and share who we are, *or* a fear of exposure, depending entirely on how we feel in the dream. If it embarrasses us to think of eliminating waste in public, it may mean we are ashamed of an aspect of our lives and want to cover it up.

Nightmares and recurring dreams which often take nightmare form usually involve us in the same dream activities I have just described but, in addition, create so much terror and tension that we wake up with hearts thumping, gasping for breath. Any fear or apprehension we may have awake will be exaggerated in a nightmare. So we run for, but *miss* the train, plane, bus or very important appointment. We *try* to run, but cannot, because our feet remain glued to the ground – or our legs will not move because they are encased in mud, cement or water. We may be paralysed from the waist down; we may call for help or give a speech and no sound emerges. We must present information to the government or the news on TV and our notes fly away. Our hair and teeth fall out; our faces crack and shatter like broken masks. We forget where we live, or where we parked the car. We drive cars with brakes that suddenly fail; we fly or climb mountains and suddenly fall to earth. We are chased, imprisoned, suffocated, or in some way threatened by such a monstrous figure or overwhelming calamity that we wake up to get away.

These dreams have an underlying sense of insecurity to them – anxiety and fear that we will not measure up to or successfully achieve other people's expectations of us. Such dreams are very common to TV announcers, radio presenters, actors and actresses – in fact to anyone performing in public. Aside from indicating an insecurity about what we do, they can also nudge us to prepare better for a particular task.

The best way of dealing with any form of nightmare or dream threat is to get back into it as quickly as possible and face it. Imagine being in the dream again. Confront the monster or threat and point your finger, a crystal, a ray of colour, love or light at it until it shrinks to a manageable size. Remember that you are dealing with emotional energy that is often suppressed when awake and exaggerated in dreams. Once it is small enough to pick up, hold and question it; 'Who are you? What are you? What part of me do you represent? How can I heal or help you? How can you help me?' Confront and conquer the threat rather than run away from it. Children who are taught to do this with dreams learn that in life, by facing what appears to be a threat, they can shrink it to a manageable size or, in other words, overcome it. If this is not possible within the dream setting, to visualize doing it while awake produces the same result.

DREAM PEOPLE

The cast of characters in our dreams – from the nasty and mean to the nice and wonderful – highlight good, bad and indifferent parts of ourselves, no matter what secondary meaning they may have. They bring to our attention characteristics we dislike, are unaware of or need to honour and acknowledge. To enter into dialogue with dream people, whether known or unknown in waking life, can help us explore the dynamics of everyday relationships. One way in which to do this is to choose a particular character and ask them: 'Who are you? Why are you in my dream? What are you doing there? What do you want me to know – about you; about me? How can we help one another?'

People in dreams often help us to audition and rehearse for waking-life situations. Dreams in which people's appearance changes dramatically – such as their teeth falling out or their faces crumbling – can indicate a fear of ageing, loss of sexuality or any other kind of attractiveness, or that we are losing our grip on a situation (re teeth) *or* the need to let go of any kind of façade regarding how we present ourselves to others. (Falling teeth dreams may even suggest the need to see a dentist!) If we witness a figure who either attacks or kills, or find (within the dream scenario) that we are doing likewise, it usually signifies killing off an aspect of ourselves that is either destructive and no longer serves our need to grow and develop, or cutting off an influence such as a parent or teacher that we need to move away from.

Jim, for example, dreamed of shooting Margaret Thatcher with a gun that fired a barrage of words rather than bullets. For him, Thatcher as a dream symbol represented 'the Iron Lady' – powerful, dictatorial and self-opinionated. This reminded him of his Greek mother-in-law who ruled his and his wife's life with an iron rod. Because he loved his wife, Jim had silently put up with this while inwardly simmering with resentment. The dream encouraged him to stand up for himself, speak out and 'shoot her down' when she became too interfering and dictatorial. It also made Jim look at how he expressed his own feminine side and he realized that he too, could be self-opinionated and dictatorial in certain situations and needed to 'shoot down' that tendency.

No matter who appears in our dreams we must always first look for the quality within ourselves that our dreams have chosen to disguise with the image of someone else. Also, noting the people who are consistently part of our waking lives, and what they symbolize or represent to us, can help clarify their presence in our dreams. Remember, though, that one week your husband may symbolize love and joy, but if you have quarrelled he may become the beast. Your children could be innocence, vulnerability, playfulness on Monday and by Friday have turned into destructive devils. When we describe other people's characters and personality traits it does not mean they are necessarily exactly like that – especially so if they are famous but unknown on a personal basis. Similarly, to dream of people from the past, especially those we have been close to, can symbolize characteristics we have taken on from them, whereas if we dream of people from the present they usually represent how we ourselves feel about them.

In short, whether looking at king, queen, president, TV announcer, postman, dustman or movie star, look at why your unconscious has chosen to project that particular image on your dream screen. What is that person doing, saying and feeling, and what is that telling you about yourself?

We can explore dream symbols, whether living or inanimate, in virtually the same way that we investigate any other parts of the dream. If, say, a hat, a wire coat-hanger and a pair of scissors appear as dream objects, we must assess whether they fit in with the general theme or seem completely out of place. And why? What do we associate these objects with in waking life? Do we use them ourselves? All the time? Occasionally? I might sum up 'hat' as 'frivolous', if I associate it with Ascot, racing, gambling and champagne picnics, but on the other hand I might connect it with sunny beaches, mountain skiing or church weddings and funerals, depending on what type of hat it is. I might assess 'wire coat-hanger' as 'inadequate' or 'inferior' if I prefer padded hangers, or as something to do with dry-cleaners or hotel or theatre cloakrooms. Scissors could imply surgery, sewing, cutting through, hair-cut, sore fingers, severing or separating, toe-nails etc. Whatever my understanding, I must then apply it to my life.

If, by chance, you cannot think what a pink elephant holding a spiky green cactus plant in its trunk in the driver's seat of your car while you sit in the back means, *ask* questions of it. 'What are you doing in my dream? Who are you? What part of me do you represent? What do you want me to know – about you; about me; What does the green cactus symbolize? How do you feel driving my car?' (You can even question the car.) Keep questioning until answers begin to pop up. With practice it becomes very easy.

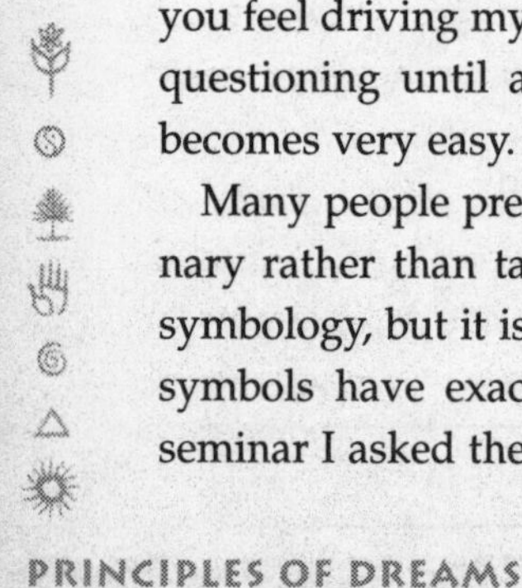

Many people prefer to consult a dream interpretation dictionary rather than take the time to work out their own dream symbology, but it is completely illogical to imagine that dream symbols have exact and invariable meanings. In one dream seminar I asked the participants to say, in a word or two, what 'bed' implied to them. These are some of the words that came up: 'repose', 'escape', 'sex', 'foundation', 'frustration', 'sleep', 'luxury', 'discomfort', 'not enough', 'imprisonment' (from someone bedridden), 'hospital', 'birth', 'sick', 'ill-health', 'warmth', 'squashed', 'retreat', 'fear', 'freedom', 'sleeplessness', 'hard work' (from a hotel maid who had to make dozens of beds a day), 'sheets', 'too small', 'big', 'obstructive' (from a girl with little space for a bed), 'excitement', 'companionship', 'love', 'family', 'cold' and 'embarrassment' (from someone who had to share their parents' bed until a teenager). Each person had a different association to the word 'bed'. It is also quite likely that 12 months later their descriptive words might completely change.

So, people who choose to interpret any part of a dream from a dictionary tend to get stuck with a surface meaning of the dream and therefore miss the personal waking-life material that underlies the dream's real message.

To look more closely at symbols, living symbols such as animals, flowers and plants relate to the innocent, naïve, natural, childlike parts of ourselves and connect us more deeply with the emotional side of our nature. Flowers symbolize purity, beauty, truth and perfection – heaven on Earth – and, whether in dreams or in life, lift our spirits and remind us of our spiritual origins. While every flower has its own quality and message to give, the rose is considered to be the most evolved of all flowers and can bring spiritual protection to every area in which it is placed. To see a rose or smell its fragrance in a dream is a sign of spiritual blessing.

Animals symbolize the animal, instinctive, wild, playful or domesticated side of our nature. To interpret any kind of animal, whether it be bird, beast or fish, look at what it represents to you. The wilder a dream animal is, the more likely it is that the instincts or habits it represents are out of control – especially if it is chasing you. If an animal appears to be abandoned, neglected, starving or in some other way ill-treated, what part of yourself have you also neglected?

Charles dreamed he arrived at Buckingham Palace to take tea with the Queen and found four or five emaciated corgis at her feet. Astounded that the Queen's dogs could look like this, he pointed to them and said, 'Ma'am, how could you neglect them so badly?' He later realized the dream was pointing at how his own slightly magisterial attitude to life had starved the joyful, spontaneous, playful parts of himself. The shock and sadness he felt in the dream encouraged him to make changes and drop some of his inherited 'queen-like' responsibilities and have more fun. To interpret any dream animal – a wily monkey, a domesticated cat, dog or chicken, a dolphin, goldfish or lobster, a snake or tree-frog – look at what it represents to you at the time of the dream. From a dove to a vulture, a snake to a rabbit, everything has its own meaning, which will be different to each one of us, depending on the thoughts and feelings we associate with it.

As I said at the beginning of this chapter, there are numerous ways of using dreams to gain understanding of our lives. Dream dialogue, whether done mentally, or through visualization, or by writing questions and answers on paper, or by listing the cast of dream characters and what they want to say, is but one way of creating an opportunity to interact with our inner life and gaining greater self-knowledge.

THE GESTALT METHOD

Similar to dream dialogue is the Gestalt method, developed by Fritz Perls, a Freudian analyst, who stripped dream interpretation of its psychological mystique and made dreamwork easy and available for everyone. Gestalt comes from the German word which means 'whole' or 'complete'. Perls saw every image and symbol as an alienated part of the personality and believed it was essential to discover and integrate them to make the person complete. In this way the parts' energy would become positive and helpful rather than destructive.

Gestalt dream therapy is one in which the dreamer tells their dream in the first person and present tense. This helps to bring the dream and its emotions to life. The dreamer then takes the part of each dream image, voices its message and states what it represents.

Gestalt is as applicable to waking life as to dreams and can give us incredible insight into other people by allowing us to imaginatively 'step into their shoes'.

Gestalt techniques can also be extremely useful in working with nightmares. If, in a dream, I am chased by a huge man wielding an axe and wake in panic, I can review the dream, imagine being inside or at one with the man and may then discover that he only chased me to protect me, or to lend me his powers or to draw attention to himself or to make me aware that I run away from my own power or ability to axe, or cut through, things.

Gestalt pushes us to confront and integrate each aspect of a dream by using chairs, cushions, or any other object to symbolize each image and move between them, asking each one to express its views until the dream's full meaning is uncovered.

OTHER METHODS ...

Dream re-entry, where awake but with eyes closed, we re-experience the dream and bring it to completion, if it is unfinished, or roll it backwards, like rewinding a video, if we want to know where or how it started, is another way to work with dreams. Again, this can be especially helpful in coming to grips with nightmares and recurring dreams.

If you feel more inclined to paint, draw, scribble or scrawl dream images rather than write or visualize them, pick an image or feeling that in some way speaks to you more than anything else in the dream and then draw, paint or make a collage of the essence of it. It does not need to be an exact picture. As well as using art as a way of recording and recalling dreams, we can use a dream picture in the same way that we might a dream symbol. Study it, immerse yourself in it. Imagine talking to it, being inside it, feeling its energy, the effect of its colours. If it could speak, what would it say? As in dream dialogue, allow thoughts, words, feelings and insights to float to the surface – without judgement. Meditate on your dreaming and leave it around where you can see it easily and often. Draw or create it again a few weeks later and see if it has changed in any way. Do not try to force meaning on any picture or symbol. Allow it to reveal its message in its own way.

Other ways of exploring dreams include 'dancing the dream alive', or using massage and bodywork, or dream sculpture – in which different people act out various parts of the dream (similar to the Gestalt technique) – or dream association, dream interview (as per Gayle Delaney) and dream incubation as well as writing, painting, drawing, music and exercise. All these can bring about dream understanding. Because some of these methods, although highly successful, can take time, I will close this chapter with a very simple technique I use myself almost every day.

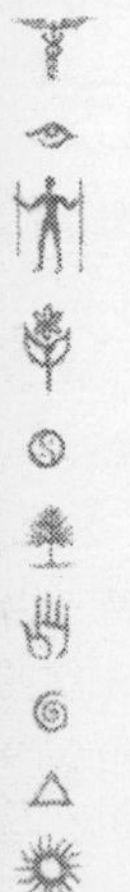

Take three major points from a dream and describe, in a word, or as briefly as possible, what each one means to you. Then write a sentence which combines the *meanings* of – but does not include – the key points themselves. Do this spontaneously and intuitively and disconnect it from the dream story. The sentence does *not* have to make logical sense. Then reduce the sentence to one word that for *you*, sums up its overall meaning. This may introduce a word that is not part of the original sentence; it does not matter. Then add 'I am' before it.

This method can be applied to dreams or waking life and allows unknown feelings to come to the surface, from which we can create a positive affirmation for life. If the result is negative, we must acknowledge the negativity but then reverse it into something positive.

Steven dreamed he walked into Buckingham Palace where the Queen ushered him into the garden. Prince Philip, dressed in a white naval uniform, heavily decorated with medals, stood beside an enormous aquamarine swimming-pool. Steven pushed him into the water and, when the Prince emerged dripping wet, pushed him in again, then a third time. Steven's three major points were:

Uniform	façade
Push	force
Water	emotions

Around these he created the sentence: 'I must force myself to drop the façade behind which I hide my feelings.' Steven also came up with 'I am sensitive', but later decided it made him feel too vulnerable (the reason he had created the façade in the first place) and changed it to 'I am expressive.'

This is *not* dream interpretation, but a way of creating an affirmation, or an ideal to strive for, that brings the dream energy into the day. We then, consciously or unconsciously, draw on this energy in applying the affirmation to our lives. This is far more effective than any affirmation or ideal that we pick out of a book. It is *not* dream interpretation, because once the three most striking words or parts of the dream are removed, they stand on their own, no longer part of the dream, but part of reality. So we can use this method to work with our own dreams and other people's dreams as well as waking-life scenarios.

Steven's dream prompted Gerald, an 80-year-old ex-soldier, to choose as his key points:

Buckingham Palace	old history/past tradition
Garden	new life – growth
Medals	achievement

His sentence was: 'I am hidebound by outdated traditions and past achievements and must now grow into a new life.' His word was 'life', his affirmation, 'I am life.'

Gerald could have created a sentence such as: 'Too much focus on my past achievements, which are now old history, blocks new ideas, growth and life.' His affirmation could have been 'I am stuck', 'I am blocked' or 'I am old'. An unconscious part of Gerald, however, pushed him to move beyond thoughts of death or the past and gave him a new lease of life.

If, in this exercise, we do end up with 'I am blocked/ stuck/afraid', we must change it to the opposite and in every waking-life situation that causes us to feel stuck or blocked, if we affirm 'I am free/fearless/powerful', the dream energy will flow to our aid.

Joy, a model, using the same dream, picked:

Queen	glamour
Philip	stuck in role
Pool	release

Her sentence was: 'I must step out of, or release myself from, my need to play the glamour queen, and be myself.' Her affirmation: 'I am who I am.'

This simple, and very quick, exercise allows us to discover a feeling or attitude about our own lives. We can expand it to include many more aspects of the dream, or review what we came up with a few months after our original assessment and redo it. It can provide a platform for deep insight and understanding, but we must then apply this to everyday life.

Steven did this by stopping wearing formal suits to work every day – unless he had important appointments – and making time to listen to his employees' problems. Gerald volunteered to take children from a local orphanage to the park two or three times a week. The children and their activities introduced him into a new way of life – they literally woke him out of his previous stagnation. Joy will always be glamorous, but decided it was not the most important thing in her life to wear matching lipstick and nail polish, or the most fashionable clothes. She took a part-time job 'granny-sitting' and the life stories she heard softened and changed her.

To actualize your dreams and bring their wisdom into the day, even if it is only to wear the colours, listen to the music or greet the person of the dream, means that you are beginning to take responsibility for what you know.

As George Bernard Shaw said, 'Other people see things and say "Why?" But I dream things and say, "Why not?" '

DREAM INTERPRETATION

Freud once said, 'The dreamer does know what his dream means, only he does not know that he knows it and, for that reason, thinks he does not know it.'

Many of us fit Freud's description. To gain understanding of our dreams we prefer to trust a 'qualified dream expert', the local psychic, Tarot or rune reader, a friend or a book – anybody or anything except ourselves. And yet, because a dream is an intimate communication from the soul to the personality, only the dreamer can decipher and truly know their own dreams. Another person's insight may catalyse a deeper or different understanding, but it is coloured by the dreamer's own experience, perception and prejudice. A dream is like a psychic reading, an encoded message unique to the dreamer and therefore we must never rest exclusively on someone else's interpretation.

Having said this, in the appendix I introduce a basic range of meanings for a variety of symbols compiled from my own dream experience and those of other people whose dreams I have investigated. I must stress, however, that no matter how universal dream symbols appear to be, they are an exclusive expression of the person who dreams them and should be interpreted as such. Antique, for example, may officially mean 'old, valuable, out of date, Sotheby's, past, history'. But for me, antique immediately reminds me of my grandmother's passion for old furniture, auctions and sales-rooms, my grandmother's house, overflowing with antique furniture, and her rage when I spilled ice-cream on a treasured dining-room table. I believe that it is more important to initially sum up a dream's overall meaning and then look at what we associate with each image, action and feeling than to focus on the literal interpretation of each word. What do the dream's images remind us of? Water will have a totally different meaning and association to a person who drinks a lot of it than to someone who has nearly drowned, for example.

Record major colours and symbols and see if there is a particular dream theme, colour, symbol or number that corresponds. Black-and-white dreams tend to be drier – more intellectual – whereas colourful dreams suggest emotion and creativity.

Always first note the numbers, figures of speech, colours, puns and names in a dream. Aside from looking up what two, three or 22 may mean numerologically, I have found the following exercise helpful in working with dream numbers. I dream, say, of the number six. Then I mentally review where I was and what I was doing six years ago. I re-run my own self-created movie, acknowledging the person I was then with a hug and an affirmation 'I love you', if it was a box-office success. If it was not a box-office success, I mentally recreate whatever occurred, but again complete the scene with a hug and an assurance of love. I then go back to when I was six and review that period of my life in exactly the same way. I either re-affirm, congratulate and reassure the child I was then, or recreate the situation if it was difficult or unhappy. This is neither numerology nor dream interpretation, but does inspire a sense of healing and happiness.

Many therapists use Active Imagination to help clients clarify their dreams. Similar to Gestalt (see page 129), Active Imagination means talking to the images that appear in one's imagination as well as entering the activities that take place. Robert Johnson, the well known Jungian analyst, said about Active Imagination, 'We confront the powerful personalities who live inside us at our unconscious level and who are so often in conflict with our conscious ideas and behaviour.' Active Imagination brings together conscious and unconscious and really means conscious participation with unconscious images.

Another way to gain understanding of dreams is to assess or review them from different levels. After noting the dream theme and key points, analyse it using left-brain logic and then right-brain intuition. To do this, close your eyes, take a few deep breaths and focus on your head. Imagine a barrier separating left and right brain, literally dividing your head in half. Move your awareness into the left side. Imagine being inside it. Is it comfortable? Colourful? Free? Dark? Empty? Constrictive?

When you have a sense of it mentally, review the dream and imagine what your logical side might say about it. Do not judge any thoughts or words that come, simply be aware of them and, opening your eyes, write them down. Then shrug your shoulders, shake your head a little, close your eyes again and do exactly the same with your right brain. Imagine being inside it, sense as much as you can and intuitively assess the dream's message from the right side of the brain. Open your eyes and write it down.

A similar procedure is to assess a dream from a physical, mental, emotional and spiritual point of view. In this case, again with your eyes closed, simply ask yourself, one at a time 'What do my physical senses … my mental senses … emotional … and spiritual … have to say about this dream?' To deepen the exercise, you could imagine a symbol for your physical body and from within it, briefly review the dream and assess the physical body's reaction to it. Then imagine a symbol for the mental body. Imagine and be inside each body symbol in turn. Note the words, thoughts, ideas and feelings that come and then imagine all the bodies merging together and light pouring into them. (This can be a very healing and centring experience on its own, even without using it for a dream assessment.)

Remember that every dream can have two, three or more interpretations or messages, and, by looking at dreams from different angles, we can greatly expand our understanding of them. I sometimes look at my own dreams from different chakra levels and find this not only broadens what I thought was the basic dream message, but can also give totally different, and often completely unexpected, insights. To do this, focus on each chakra in turn – it does not matter if you go from base to crown or crown to base. You may even prefer to pick only one or two chakras at a time instead of going through them all at once. Again with your eyes closed, imagine each chakra and its qualities and review how each level might assess the dream. The root or base chakra, associated with survival, the physical and material worlds, would no doubt assess a dream's message quite differently from the third eye chakra, which connects us to invisible worlds and is the seat of intuition and imagination. I described the chakras and their qualities in Chapter 7, but here is a brief reminder:

Chakra	*Colour*	*Quality*
root or base	red	survival, physical sensation
spleen or sacral	orange	instinctive emotion
solar plexus	yellow	communication
heart	green	love
throat	blue	authority, identity
third eye	indigo	intuition, imagination
crown	violet	spiritual understanding

With any of these exercises do not be afraid of making a mistake. Say to yourself, 'This is the way I *currently* understand my dream. Tomorrow, next month or next year I may understand it differently.'

Dreamwork and dream interpretation should be simple, practical and, above all, fun, helping us to opt into life rather than to cut off from it. Do not let any of the suggestions in this book become a burden, but rather use or adapt what works for you and drop the rest. If there is not enough time to record a dream each day, note the one you still remember two or three days later. Instead of analysing, or working with, every dream, pick one a week or a month or every six months. When a dream hits the spot, when every cell in your body tingles, you will automatically integrate its wisdom into your life.

A dream is a secret conversation, a friendly communication between our waking selves and soul selves. As such, some dreams do not lend themselves to interpretation but, by simply letting them float around in our minds, they affect us. For myself, the guarantee of a dream's importance is both the emotional impact within the dream and the electrifying burst of energy with which I wake up to implement the dream's message. Even without specific interpretation I believe a dream has been truly understood and integrated when one's life changes as a result.

Geoffrey Winthrop Young, a great mountaineer who lost a leg in the First World War and then climbed the Matterhorn with an artificial leg, wrote a poem from which I plucked the following:

> 'I have not lost the magic of long days,
> I live them still, dream them still …
> With dreams I charmed each doing to delight,
> I keep the dreams, I keep the dreams I won …
> I dream my feet upon the starry ways …
> I may not grudge the little left undone.
> I hold the heights, I keep the dreams I won.'

May you too, dream the magic of long days, walk the starry ways and keep the dreams you won.

GROUP DREAMING

> Speak your truth quietly and clearly; and listen to others, even to the dull and the ignorant; they too have their story.
>
> DESIDERATA

Since I was a child the world of dreams has always fascinated me. I was, and still am, a prolific dreamer with a good dream memory, so in some way or another I would try to record them. Initially I made clumsy attempts to draw or paint the animals, figures, shapes and faces that filled my dreams and sometimes cut them out and propped them up, like miniature actors set in place for a play or a movie. I was not a doll-lover, but tolerated Victoria, a large china doll with limpid brown eyes, who appeared to listen intently to my tales of flying unicorns, Tinker Bell type fairies,winged angels and fat pink snakes that slithered horribly about both in and under my bed. But when my brother overheard some of these discussions, and then discovered my primitive artistic efforts, he teased and tormented me so much that I became very secretive about my dream life.

Later, when I was six and despatched from Sri Lanka to boarding-school in England, dreams helped me to cope with my almost unbearable terror, unhappiness and loneliness. They were my secret source of survival and I spent hours writing them down in miniscule script, often by torchlight under the bedclothes to avoid discovery. Until I was in my early twenties my dreams were strictly private conversations between my inner and my outer self. I would have been more comfortable running naked across a football pitch than revealing my dream journals to another human being. The idea of sharing dreams with a group never even crossed my mind – not because my dreams were sexually explicit or shamefully violent, but simply because they were an aspect of my own inner being that I rarely shared with anyone.

I did, however, stimulate my dreaming brain by reading dozens of books on Freud, Jung, Edgar Cayce and numerous other great and famous dream explorers, and I discovered that around the world there are dream clubs, groups, newsletters, magazines, research centres, workshops, seminars and lectures through which dreamers can share their dreams. Eventually, after attending my first dream seminar, I realized that dream-sharing gives dreams more importance to both our waking and sleeping minds, helps stimulate dream recall, and amplifies and enriches our understanding of dreams in a way that I had not imagined possible.

Later I spent time with Africans, Native Americans and Australian aborigines and saw that communal dream discussion helped develop a wisdom which, when acted upon, empowered and transformed tribal life. As Jeremy Taylor, the American priest and dream expert, says, 'When the multiple intelligences and intuitions of several people are brought to bear on a dream, or a series of dreams, it is much more likely that the dreamer will be exposed to a fuller range of the dreams' possible meaning.'

This is exactly why dream groups are so popular. Other people's comments and insight help shed extra light on dreams, even though they are still in every sense unique to the dreamer, even when common themes or symbols are present. To speak a dream aloud is quite different from writing it down and, in my experience, allows the dream-sharers to feel into the dream in a different way. This can also show how changed our dream language may be when asleep compared to when awake.

Sharing dreams with a husband, wife, lover or friend can lead to deeper understanding, better communication, and insight into unresolved issues, as well as greater love and harmony. As I mentioned before, family dream-sharing is a wonderful way to encourage children to value their dreams and express feelings they may otherwise hide – especially when this includes enacting the dreams or keeping them alive through some form of simple artwork.

At one time I used to have groups of children at my house every Saturday morning for eight consecutive weeks – similar to the average school term. Although we did many different things, dreamwork was one of the popular. Each child shared dreams, nightmares, fears and problems. We practised the dream breathing exercise (see page 22), wrote stories, painted pictures, made collages, sand-paintings and plasticine models of dream figures and sometimes acted out the characters of different dreams. During that period my own dreams were extraordinarily vivid – in fact I notice this occurs whenever I give a dream seminar.

After two or three weeks some of the parents began to telephone to ask exactly what went on in these classes. Fearing problems, I was a little apprehensive when I told them, and was amazed to learn that a number of children's attitudes, both at home and at school, had improved dramatically.

Another way to encourage children's dreams is to read them stories and ask them which part they would like to play. This can be just as successful with one child as with 20. One child or six can play Cinderella, the Prince or the Ugly Sisters – they can each act part of a story in turn and then swap. Anything we can do to stir the imagination of children – and adults – has an effect on dreams. The more we can help each other to accept the hidden aspects of our psyches revealed in dreams, and then integrate these parts into our everyday life, the happier, healthier and more whole we become. To begin to do this in childhood gives us a far better chance of living emotionally balanced lives as adults.

My first dream-sharing group began with six like-minded (or dream-minded) friends. We met once a week for eight weeks in my tiny Sydney apartment. For three hours we discussed and attempted to analyse the stuff of our dreams, often with moving and sometimes hilarious results. We read up, and practised on one another, dream association, analogy, metaphoric symbology, and the differences between coloured and black-and-white dreams. We studied books with titles such as *How Do We Know That Dreams Have Meaning?* and solemnly pronounced statements by Jung that began with phrases such as 'In each of us there is another whom we do not know. He speaks to us in dreams and tells us how differently he sees us from the way we see ourselves… ' or 'A dream is too slender a hint to be understood until it is enriched by the stuff of associations and analogy and thus amplified to the point of intelligibility…'

For Jung the purpose of dream interpretation was the dreamer's psychological development. He suggested four tests to apply to the truth of an interpretation:

1. Does the interpretation 'click' with the dreamer?
2. Does the interpretation 'act' for (or give new energy to) the dreamer?
3. Is the interpretation confirmed by subsequent dreams?
4. Do the events predicted in a dream occur in waking life?

Jung also described how the different functions of sensation, thinking, feeling and intuition distinguished one person from another because in each, one function is better developed than the others. He defined these as follows: 'Sensation tells you that something exists; thinking tells you what it is; feeling tells you whether it is agreeable or not; and intuition tells you where it comes from and where it is going.' Jung observed that when thinking is the best developed function, feeling is likely to be the weakest, and when sensation is the most developed, intuition tends to be weak, and vice versa.

Our dream group applied and adapted everything we read as best we could and we developed a deep understanding of one another, which so enriched our lives that we continued to meet for another 12 months. Finally, events such as marriage, a change of job or house, the birth of a baby or new interests brought our meetings to a close.

This simple introduction to group work eventually led to my speaking in public, giving weekend and week-long seminars, individual therapy and 30–40 day retreats cum holiday workshops. I began to compile a list of basic requirements for successful group dream work – although it can of course be adapted to any other subject.

First, decide on the size of the group. If you have 20, 30 or more friends and acquaintances, all mad keen to study their dreams, you may want to invite a professional dream therapist to preside. In this case the group must be prepared to pay a fee, which not only covers the hours involved but also the therapist's travel expenses. Most therapists cannot afford, either financially or time-wise, to come once a week every week for two or three hours to a small village well off the beaten track. To make this idea feasible it is better to consider a once a month or a once every two or three months day-long seminar – or even a once or twice a year weekend seminar, depending on the therapist's fee and what the group can afford. In between the professional's visits, those who want to can organize small weekly meetings or work in pairs with one another.

If you begin, as I did, with a few friends, be sure in your own mind that they are completely trustworthy, in the sense that they will not gossip about anything that comes up during a dream session. Sometimes what arises is intensely personal and private. Also ensure that each person is willing to commit to attending regularly – except of course in the case of unexpected emergency. This means that there must be a mutual agreement between all group members how often these meetings will take place. It is no good agreeing in a burst of initial enthusiasm to meet every week if the attendance thereafter is sporadic. If you start with weekly meetings and later realize that some people can only commit themselves to once a month either change the schedule by consensus or let those who are unwilling, or unable, to attend regularly drop out. When members of a group drift in and out, no solid foundation is formed. It is better to have, for example, three eight-week segments a year, with time off in between, than to create a schedule which is impossible to keep.

Be careful about numbers – avoid having so many that each member cannot share their dreams regularly. It is usually impossible for everyone to share a dream in one evening, so it is better to allow the time to work with one or two dreams each time you meet than try to deal with too many all at once. Get each group member to recount a dream or two in turn – this week Annie, next week Andrew, etc. Allow enough time for discussion and group work after each dream is related.

Next decide the meeting-place. A small group – I believe that the basic minimum should be four to six – can meet in someone's house, while if there are 50 plus of you, you may need to hire a hall. If you meet in someone's house, will it be the same house every week or will you take it in turns to be the host? Plan, and let everyone know beforehand, to avoid confusion.

Many people flinch at the idea of charging a fee, especially for a small intimate group meeting in one's own house. In my experience, however, a small donation from each person helps solidify the group purpose. The money can be used for tea, coffee and biscuits, or materials such as paper, books and tapes, or even given to charity.

Choose the times to start and stop and stick to them. Group work requires a commitment to the group as well as to the subject in hand and if people trail in and out whenever they feel like it, nothing worthwhile can develop.

Before you start, set an ideal for the group. What does each person hope to get out of it – and to put into it? What is the overall aim? This helps to focus the group energy as well as clarifying to each person why they are there.

At the first meeting it is helpful if each person shares not only why they are there but also offers a brief summary of their life. Dependent on time, life-story telling can amount to five minutes, or, in month-long workshops, we sometimes take an entire week to listen to each person's life story. This helps to clear them out of the teller's systems and to remind us that we all have basically the same story of griefs, hopes, fears, joys, accomplishment and failure. These stories usually stimulate incredible dreams, so that the dream becomes the life story and the life story the dream, and light is shed on both.

Create an atmosphere of peace, tranquillity and trust by opening and closing each session or meeting with a moment of attunement. This can be done by lighting a candle and holding hands around it; chanting sounds, such as *Om*; sitting in silence, while aligning to love, truth and inspiration; invoking through prayer the presence of specific angels; cleansing the aura; prayer; meditation; breathing in light and breathing out negativity; or any form of visualization exercises or chanting. All these help to loosen people – mentally, physically and imaginatively – so that answers and images float in more easily.

When listening to other people sharing their dreams, listen not only to their story but also to their words and tone of voice. Do not interrupt. Watch their body language and notice how your own body and emotions react. Rather than what you think a dream is saying to the dreamer, *feel* what the dream says to you, as if it were your dream. When these feelings and insights are shared, they can give the dreamer an expanded understanding of their own dream.

Take it in turns to lead and even if a professional dream therapist guides the group, let them also share and work with their dreams within the group.

Do not get fixed with any one specific way of working with dreams. Explore together dream incubation, lucid dreaming, past, present, future and collective dreaming, vision quests, astral travel ... Read books, go to lectures, amplify your dreams through art, music, acting or anything else that unfolds your own inner wisdom.

If someone has great difficulty in remembering dreams, especially at initial meetings, suggest they describe a favourite book, film or television play as if it were their dream. Then let the group members help the person to explore why this story is so meaningful by questioning them. It can also help, when starting off, to have a story read aloud, or to listen to a taped story, and let each person work with it as if it were their own personal dream. After five or ten minutes, ask each member to share what message they have picked up in relation to their own personal daily life. When doing this, do not try and interpret, in a literal sense, each piece of the story, but rather let each individual pick out what has more impact and then *intuitively* guess what the message is.

Another exercise that works well in a group is to ask one person to share a dream, while everyone listens with their eyes closed. Let the guide or leader note the dream story at the third telling – drop the first two, which are often different from the last. The leader then guides the group through the dream as if it were a visualization exercise. The group, including the dreamer, listen with closed eyes. The leader then questions the dreamer as to their association with different dream elements –'What did you feel?' What do these feelings remind you of in waking life?'' What part of you do the cat and the monkey represent?' 'Who does XYZ remind you of?' – using the format described in previous chapters and including any question that pops into the leader's mind. The dreamer answers the questions aloud, while the group either mentally answers the questions – from each person's personal perspective – or notes them on paper. Always conclude with what the dream appears to say to each person and how it can be applied to waking life.

Then let everyone share. This exercise stimulates each person's understanding of their own dream.

Another popular exercise is to have the group pair off, take it in turns to listen to one another's dream and then guide it forwards or backwards, using dream re-entry.

If group members are initially shy about sharing details of their lives, the following exercise is fun, can give surprising insight, creates a strong group dynamic and triggers the brain's ability to read symbols.

Have everyone bring as many old colourful, picture-filled magazines as possible, a pair of scissors, a pot of glue or paste and an A4 envelope. After an attunement and a few deep breaths through which to leave the day and the outside world aside, the leader asks everyone to reflect briefly on 'Who am I? What are the main aspects of myself I would like others to know about?' Now everyone opens their eyes and has *five* minutes to grab some magazines, quickly scan them for any picture that symbolizes something of their personality, likes and dislikes, work, lifestyle, favourite holidays, pastimes, food, etc., and tear them out. After the five minutes are up, remove the magazines and give the group another five minutes to cut out their pictures neatly and make a collage with them on the *front* of the envelope. After five minutes they *must* stop, even if some of the chosen pictures remain unglued to the envelope. They now have *two* minutes to stick any remaining pictures on the back. Again, as soon as two minutes are up, they must stop and place any leftover pictures inside the envelope. Each person now takes a partner and swaps envelopes with them. After a few moments to assess the front of one another's envelopes, Partner A tells Partner B what they feel their collage says about them. Allow each partner three minutes to share, one at a time. The partner who is listening must do so without interruption. Then each partner takes two minutes to share what they sense from the pictures on the back of the envelope, and then inside the envelope. Are they similar or very different? When both envelopes have been examined, front , back and inside, and *without mutual discussion* as to the accuracy of the personality diagnosis, let each person introduce their partner to the group, from their 'envelope assessment', no matter how accurate or inaccurate it might be. Only after each person in the group has introduced their partner should the pairs take time to discuss with each other how they felt about each other's diagnosis.

The front of the envelope symbolizes the outer expression of the personality; the back symbolizes a side not immediately revealed, while the pictures inside reflect the hidden, interior world. Some people put everything on the front and nothing on the back, while others place a plethora of pictures inside and virtually nothing anywhere else. This is neither good nor bad, but simply reflects the state of consciousness at the time. It is better not to give too detailed a description of what the front, back and inside of the envelope mean beforehand, as it can spoil the spontaneity. This is also why very little time is given for each part.

After a few weeks of meetings, it is helpful to have a session in which, instead of group discussion, the group devotes time to making a mandala or shield of power, using key symbols, colours, animals and flowers from the dreams that have been shared. This could be a joint effort, with everyone contributing to one mandala or picture, or each person could create their own. When this is done from a series of dreams rather than just one, it lays before the group, collectively and individually, the story of their unfolding wisdom and can become a source of energy. Because it brings together conscious and unconscious, it stimulates one to act upon the other.

Remember, too, that guided visualization exercises always stimulate the conscious and unconscious to co-operate. These should be preceded by deep relaxation, in which we meet a dream master, imagine a temple or house of dreams, communicate with an angel or personal teacher and guide who will help us understand our dreams.

Some groups like to record their sessions on tape. Others prefer to make personal notes throughout, or have one person note down key points which are photocopied for everyone else afterwards. Others prefer to take their impression away in their heads and record any relevant information at home. It does not matter what a particular group does as long as it works for them.

Once your group is under way, try and allow time at the beginning of each meeting for members to share what has come up for them in their waking life as the result of dreams discussed with the group. The only problem with this is that it can take too long, so it may be better just to ask the person whose

dream was the main focus of the previous week's session to give a brief summary or check in. If this proves too time-consuming, assign one complete session at regular intervals when everyone discusses any life changes since the dreamwork began.

Bear in mind that every dream and every symbol has multiple meanings, never be afraid of what may be revealed and, above all, have fun. Remember angels can fly because they take themselves lightly.

APPENDIX

UNDERSTANDING DREAM SYMBOLS

Accident	A warning to slow down; not paying enough attention
Acorn	Good luck. A reminder to nurture your own 'seed of potential'.
Actor	How you see yourself/others see you. The role you play.
Addict	Giving up power. Fear of life and expressing the real self.
Aeroplane	Expansion. Elevated consciousness. The ability to 'fly high'.
Air	Freedom, the breath of life.
Alcohol	Denial of the self, of life. Escape, illusion, giving away power.
Anchor	Commitment, a need to anchor the self or resistance to being tied.
Angel	Protection, guidance, love.
Animal	The animal or instinctual side of nature. By absorbing the energy of the animal symbol we can integrate with a particular trait within our being, and then draw on its strength.
Antique	An outmoded condition, relationship, pattern or belief. Something past.
Applause	Approval from the soul and/or guides.

Arctic Animal	A frozen or undeveloped quality, symbolized by the animal.
Armour	Self-protection. Defensiveness.
Ashes	Something ended, burned out.
Attic	Higher consciousness, spiritual attainment.
Audience	A suggestion to express yourself. If unwilling to 'perform' in the dream or the audience is not listening, some part of you is resistant to what you are being invited to do.
Author	A reminder that we write our own life script and if it's not a box-office success, we can change it.
Avalanche	The loosening up of frozen emotions.
Baby	New consciousness, new awareness. A refusal to care for a baby means a refusal to take responsibility for new wisdom.
Baby-sitting	A reminder to care for new awareness or our own inner child.
Baker	Someone who shares spiritual truths.
Ball	Playing the game. Group consciousness.
Balloon	Soaring, uplifting, releasing, moving beyond the physical.
Bandage	An attempt to hide something.
Bank	A safe place, a storehouse or reservoir of energy (money is a symbol of energy exchange).
Banquet	A celebration or tendency to overindulge.
Bar	A need for spiritual comfort – fellowship, camer-aderie (i.e. *true* spirit, not just from a bottle).
Barefoot	Humility.
Barricade	Being hemmed in, blocked, at a standstill.
Basement	Subconscious.
Bath/Bathing	A time for cleansing and renewal.
Battle	Inner conflict.
Beach	Dependent on whether you are stranded or

	relaxing, this can mean you are cut off from your emotions or that it's time to take a little space for yourself.
Bed	Future work with whoever is in it, plus safety, security.
Beggar	Being dependent on others. Lack of self-reliance.
Bell	Alerts one to new experience – maybe marriage, death, or spiritual insight.
Bicycle	Balance; freedom. If you are struggling uphill, what are you putting energy into that may be misplaced?
Birds	Freedom, elevation, the ability to move in more than one dimension. Messengers of the soul. A flock of birds is telepathy.
Birth	Birth to a higher self.
Blindness	A refusal or inability to see clearly.
Blood	Life force.
Boat	The emotional body. The voyage through life.
Body	The vehicle through life – a reminder to care for it.
Book	Akashic record.
Boss	Higher self, teacher, guide.
Boulder	An obstacle to overcome.
Box	Restriction, limitation, self- or otherwise imposed.
Brakes	Faulty brakes means beginning to lose control and no brakes means loss of control. Brakes full on suggest blocking one's progress.
Bread	Communion, sacrament, sharing.
Breast	Nourishment.
Bride & Bridegroom	Balance and alignment, or merger of inner male and female, animus and anima.
Bridge	Transition.

Briefcase	Working identity – is it empty, overloaded or just right?
Broom	Sweeping or cleaning away whatever is outmoded, unnecessary.
Buds	New life.
Building	Sometimes a symbol for the body; sometimes a symbol of future potential. An unfinished building means something unresolved.
Burden	Trying to do too much.
Butterfly	Transformation. Metamorphosis. Reincarnation. Transition.
Cage	Self-limitation.
Cake	Celebration or indulgence.
Camera	Standing outside what is happening.
Candle	Inner light, will-power.
Cane/Crutch	Learning or being dependent on something or someone.
Car	The physical body. The ability to move through life. An old car equals outmoded ideas.
Cat	Psychic protection or attack, dependent on the dream. A kitten is immaturity, playfulness.
Cave	The inner self.
Chair	Support.
Cheque	Paying one's dues – not necessarily financial ones.
Children	Joy, freedom, spontaneity. One's own inner child – sometimes abandoned.
Christmas	Joy, celebration, spiritual festivity, love.
Church	Spirituality, but can also represent fixed or rigid beliefs, a lack of life.
Circle	Completion, wholeness, oneness with God.
Circus	Joy, playfulness, enjoyment.
City	Community, shared work, communication.

Cliff	Change, a move into something new. If falling off a cliff, watch your step!
Clock/Watch	Time. Too much? Too little?
Clothes	Part of your role-playing self-identity. If historical, may be a reminder of a past life. If old and worn, discard outworn parts of yourself.
Coffin	Death of a phase of life, relationship or idea.
College	The school of life, spiritual knowledge.
Colours	Each colour is a manifestation of the vibratory rate of a particular colour ray. Each ray has certain characteristics, and therefore to see colours in a dream indicates an alignment with, or need to focus on, the vibratory power (or quality of energy) contained within the colours seen. Absence of colour usually denotes absence of life, emotion and vitality.
Amber	Life force, sun.
Beige	Detachment, non-involvement, neutrality.
Black	Absence of colour and light. Indifference. Unknowing.
Black–Pink	Destructive.
Blue	Wisdom, clarity, truth, peace.
Blue, Pale	Passivity.
Blue, Turquoise	Freedom of expression.
Brown	Introverted, retreating, going inside oneself. Concealment of identity.
Green	Life, health, healing, balance.
Grey	Detachment, aloofness.
Gold	Enlightenment. Colour of God.
Indigo (Midnight/ navy blue)	Imagination, intuition. Third Eye initiation.

Lavender	Spirituality – sometimes connects to asthma or difficulty with breathing at birth.
Orange	Emotional assimilation, physical digestion, release.
Pink	Love
Purple/Violet	Transformation, spiritual responsibility, inspiration, spiritual healing.
Red	Physical energy, action, expansion. Lowest rate of vibration.
Silver	Cool, mystical, moon initiation.
White	Perfection (white light of Christ), purity. Highest rate of vibration.
Yellow	Mental power. Determination. Assessment and joy. Sun, freedom of inner child.

Convent	Retreat, withdrawal.
Cook	Sharing love, giving oneself; creativity, blending.
Court	Self-judgement.
Cow	Domesticity.
Crab	Defensiveness, escape, vulnerability.
Critic	Self-discipline.
Cross	Christ consciousness or martyrdom (usually self-inflicted).
Crossroads	Choice of direction.
Crown	Of jewels, crown chakra initiation; of thorns, martyr complex.
Crutch	*See* Cane.
Crying	Emotional release or inner solution to problem.
Crystal	True self. Purity. Clarity. Divine light.
Cup	Emotional receptivity.
Curtain	Closed – hiding self or some aspect of life; open – sharing and willingness to expose new ideas, life, etc.

Dance	Blending energy, movement, relaxation.
Death	Release, letting go, dying to the past or to old habits. A need to release the quality inherent in a person who dies. Dreams of death can sometimes also prepare one for death, either one's own or another's.
Defecation	Letting go.
Dentist	Assistance with the personality and expressing one's own truth.
Desert	Emotional aridity.
Devil	Fear. Resistance.
Diary	Self-perception.
Disease	Unease in attitude towards self. Emotional imbalance.
Doctor	Need for healing and guidance.
Dog	Loyalty, faith. (Look at breed: mongrel symbolizes mixed beliefs, poodle vanity and terrier inquisitiveness.)
Donkey	Stubbornness, or the willingness to carry burdens.
Door	Open – opportunity; closed – a block.
Dove	The Holy Spirit.
Drawers	Stored ideas. If untidy, sort out priorities.
Drowning	Difficulties threaten to overwhelm you.
Drugs	Fantasy, illusion.
Duck	Avoidance, e.g. to duck an issue.
Eagle	Daring, courage, evolution.
Earth	Firm foundation. If muddy, lack of foundation. Too dry equals lack of emotional nurturing. Grovelling in the earth is making a mess of life, abusing it.
Earthquake	Huge change, inner turmoil.
Easter	Spiritual rebirth.

Egg	Fertility, birth, new life.
Electricity	Vibrational life-force.
Elephant	Perseverance. Family. Memory.
Escape	Avoidance of self or problems. A reminder to face fears.
Exam	Initiation. If anxious in dream, fear of failure.
Explosion	The release of suppressed negativity.
Eye	The eye of God; spiritual eye. Eyes open – clarity of vision; closed – resistance to clear seeing.
Face	Face up to a situation or face yourself.
Falling	Humility, falling down on something.
Family	Integration of different parts of the self.
Fat	Self-protection – especially of emotional space.
Father	Authority and/or what the father in life represented. Can also be Heavenly Father.
Fax	The ability to communicate instantly.
Feather	Native American symbol for a blessing.
Film	Life review.
Fire	Purification. (Can sometimes predict illness.) A forest fire is a cleansing, balancing.
Fireman	Teacher, guide or higher soul self who can assist purification.
Fish	Spiritual truth, Christ consciousness. Eating fish is to partake of spiritual truths.
Fleas	*See* Flies.
Flies/Fleas/ Insects	Malice, psychic attack, negativity, parasitic people.
Flowers	Emotional expansion, spiritual grace, life. Wild flowers mean simplicity, purity. Cultivated flowers are emotional development.
Flying	The ability to use higher levels of consciousness. Expansion.
Fog	Confusion.

Food	Sharing, communion, spiritual and physical nourishment.
Foreigner	Insecurity.
Fountain	Spiritual nourishment. Female master.
Funeral	Death of the old or death of an aspect of the self.
Gambler	Taking chances – watch what you are doing.
Garage	A temporary place for rest or healing.
Garden	Consciousness. A wild garden means work to do on oneself.
Gate	New openings. If open, you accept; if closed, you block opportunity.
Giant	If threatening, fear and self-doubt, out of proportion. If co-operating, shows giant ability to succeed.
Glass	Protection, insulation. Broken glass means something finished, over.
Gloves	Handle something in your life with care.
Grass	Peace, life, health and healing.
Grave	Lost hopes, lifeless emotions.
Guest	An unfamiliar part of the self.
Guillotine	Either don't lose your head in a certain situation or chop off your tendency to live solely in the head and deny your feelings/intuition.
Gutter	Hopelessness.
Gypsy	Freedom, irresponsibility. Restlessness. Refusal to conform.
Hair	Virility. A haircut means shedding old concepts.
Handle	The ability to grasp what and who you are. If a door has no handle, a sense of inability to cope, to get a handle on something.

Hat	Protecting the role you play.
Hedge	Can be protection or the sense of being hemmed in by too much to do.
Helicopter	Overview of the past, present and future.
Hole	Something in need of repair, or a situation you have dug yourself or fallen into.
Horizon	Expansion.
Horse	Strength, progress. The energy to carry one through life.
Hospital	Restriction and a need for love, attention and physical healing.
Hotel	Transition.
House	The physical body. If a house has many floors it symbolizes different bodies, i.e. mental, spiritual emotional and physical, plus different levels of consciousness. The basement is the subconscious. The attic is the higher consciousness. The kitchen is work, sharing, needs which are being met. A bedroom means rest and renewal. Sharing a bed means working with the person in the bed. Sexuality means merging one's own qualities with those symbolized by the other person. A living-room is communication and sharing. A bathroom is the need to eliminate, cleanse, or to be in the process of so doing.
Hovel	Spiritual poverty, self-denial.
Hunger	Emotional or spiritual need for fulfilment.
Ice	Frozen condition, the need to thaw one's emotions.
Iceberg	Submerged or frozen feelings.
Ice-Cream	Indulgence.
Idiot	Foolishness, irresponsibility.

Idol	Having false values, worshipping something false – a person, material possessions.
Injection	If life saving, a need for energy; if a drug, self-destruction.
Insects	*See* Flies.
Interview	Preparation for initiation, self-discovery, self-assessment.
Invasion	Lack of personal privacy and space or fear of an invasion of one's privacy; can symbolize fear of rape.
Ironing	To sort out (iron out) problems or too many irons in the fire.
Island	Isolation, separation.
Jewels	Cut jewels signify grace, spiritual power. Uncut jewels are qualities which are waiting to be developed. (See my book *The Power of Gems and Crystals* (Piatkus, 1989) for a more detailed interpretation.) To touch a jewel is to be recharged with its quality.
Journey	The voyage through life.
Judge	Conscience, self-criticism, hidden guilt.
Juggler	Trying to do too many things at once.
Jump	A new step – look before you leap.
Key	To be ready for the next step; the answer to a problem. A bunch of keys means opening many things at once.
Kill	Destroy a negative part of your life.
Kiss	Brotherhood, brotherly love. If sensual, it shows conscious or unconscious sexual feelings between the people kissing.
Kitchen	Companionship – the heart of the house, nourishment.

Knife	Can be used to wound or heal. May suggest a need to separate, cut oneself off from an aspect of oneself or another or to prepare oneself for surgery.
Knot	A need to untie from a situation or relationship – or to strengthen the tie that binds.
Laboratory	Testing new ideas.
Ladder	Ascension.
Lake	Emotional peace – if the water is rough, emotions are disturbed and need to be balanced.
Lamb	Sacrifice, vulnerability.
Late	Fear of missing out, lost opportunities, avoidance, lack of self-worth.
Laughter	Need to relax, enjoy life. Don't take life too seriously. If people laugh at you, mock you, is what you present to them false?
Laundry	Cleansing, or the need to, of the self.
Lecture	Pay attention.
Letter	News. Communication.
Library	Knowledge. One's book of life.
Light	Enlightenment.
Lily	Resurrection, purity.
Lion	Power, ego, mastery.
Lobster	Insulation, hypersensitivity. (Shellfish generally mean a perceived need to armour oneself.)
Lock	Precaution, protection. A broken lock can mean a lack of responsibility.
Loss	Fear of losing out or actual loss.
Lost	Indecision.
Luggage	If light, not carrying one's weight. If heavy, over-burdened with responsibilities – often for others, and often unnecessary.

Machine	Lack or loss of emotional sensitivity.
Mafia	Inner conflict, manipulation by self or others.
Magician	Ability to transform or to create illusions that fool others.
Market	Multi-dimensional choices available – choose.
Marriage	Union with the higher, soul self.
Martyr	Lack of self-love.
Mask	Concealment. Ego-personality. A mask breaking or cracking can mean the opening up of the real self.
Menstruation	Release.
Messenger	Soul/higher self, guidance. Listen to inner wisdom.
Microphone	Broaden the expression of yourself and your needs.
Microscope	Self-examination.
Milk	Nourishment from the Divine Mother; spiritual truth.
Mirror	The need to face oneself.
Model	False representation of the self.
Money	Energy, the exchange of energy.
Monk	Renunciation.
Monkey	Inquisitive, playful.
Monster	Exaggerated sense of fear.
Moon	Emotions, dredging up emotions from the past.
Mother	Nurturing power of the feminine *or* 'witch-mother'; abuse, criticism.
Motor	The power to move through life, acceleration.
Mountain	An effort to develop. Climbing a mountain is a spiritual journey towards evolution.
Mud	To be physically, mentally or emotionally stuck.
Mummy	(Egyptian, not mother.) Stifled, encased in old beliefs and habits.
Murder	Annihilate what no longer serves.

Museum	Archetypal learning from past. Outdated history.
Music	Experience of music of the spheres, healing, initiation into the power of sound vibration, contact with angelic realms.
Naked	Revealing the self, ideas. Freedom.
Name	Your own or others – listen and pay attention to qualities they represent. Can also be a call from your guides to jolt you awake (in consciousness).
Necklace	Spiritual powers.
Needle	Mending one's ways.
Neighbour	Spiritual brother – understanding companion.
Nest	Desire for security.
Newspaper	Publicity, notoriety.
Nose	Being nosey or needing to know.
Numbers	
1	Will, initiative, inspiration.
2	Duality, caring, sharing, partnership.
3	Communication, expression. Trinity or three-fold aspect of God as Mother, Father and Son or will, wisdom and love.
4	Master of self and the laws of Earth. Initiation, sacrifice, karma as signified by the Cross.
5	Freedom, expansion, versatility, five-pointed star as symbol of the perfected man.
6	Balance (especially in relationships), heaven and Earth, giving, service, synthesis. Marriage, emotion and thought.
7	The number of the mystic, the seeker of truth. Someone who looks at life from a different perspective.
8	Power. Macrocosm. Microcosm.

9	Authority. Mastery over the lessons of life, overcoming challenges. Development of the higher will.
10	The completion. 'I am whole' or one with God.
11	A master number, meaning that it has added potential – as do 22, 33, 44, etc. Each has a double dose of the quality of its original number.
12	Cosmic order, discipleship, a blend of world and spirit.
Nurse	Nurturing – either needing to receive or to give.
Ocean	Emotional energy. If calm, emotional balance; if rough, emotional turbulence; if dried up, emotions also dry.
Octopus	Being drained by another sucking one's life force.
Oil	Oil from a well equals worldly support. Annointing with oil means discipleship.
Operation	Repair either being carried out or needed (not necessarily physical).
Oracle	Divination. Prophecy.
Orchestra	Bring your life into harmony.
Ostrich	Avoidance of problems or growth.
Overcoat	A need to cover up or protect.
Owl	Wisdom.
Oyster	Hiding own inner beauty.
Paintbrush	*See* Pens.
Papaya	Cleansing, balancing digestion.
Parachute	Help if we need to bail out.
Paralysis	Immobilized by fear of a situation or problem.
Parrot	Gossip. Fun, chatter, companionship.
Party	Celebration. Joy, recognition of soul partners or letting go to the lower senses.

Passenger	Not taking charge of one's own life.
Passport	Identity.
Peacock	Vanity.
Pens/Pencils/ Paintbrush	Communication. A need for self-expression. Creativity.
Perfume	Healing, blessing, angelic presence.
Phoenix	Transformation, evolution, a spiritual teacher.
Photo	Self-examination.
Pig	Greed. Sensuality.
Play	Reviewing what we have planned for ourselves – from past, present or future.
Plumbing	Elimination (if in public, means freedom). Releasing and letting go. If one is trying to find a secret place in which to act, it implies something to conceal, a sense of shame.
Police	Angelic guides or teachers, the will of God, grace, protection and/or warning. A sign of care and love.
Postman	Message from the higher self.
Pregnancy	Preparing for the birth of a new level of understanding.
President	Authority.
Price Tag	Are you willing to pay the price? Are you overdrawn at the bank – in time, emotion, energy or money?
Prison	Self-created limitation. Holding back.
Prize	Appreciation.
Prostitute	Misuse of energy to get something you want. Giving away power, abandonment to physical senses.
Puppet	Manipulation of the self or others, or by others.
Puzzle	Intricate, separated bits of self-knowledge.
Quarrel	A problem in presenting your own ideas.

Queen	The goddess within, the power of the feminine.
Quest	A spiritual journey, the search for the Holy Grail, the search for the soul.
Quicksand	Sinking into an aspect of life; rapidly becoming out of control – similar to drowning.
Quilt	Both covering up an aspect of life and creativity – especially if a patchwork quilt, which signifies joining together different aspects of ourselves.
Rabbit	Timidity.
Race	Ambition. Competition, challenge.
Radio	The ability to 'tune in', telepathic communication.
Rags	Wasted ideas and ideals.
Rain	A cleansing of emotions.
Rainbow	A sign of God and angelic protection. Celebration.
Rape	Violation of space, invasion of privacy.
Record	Either the Akashic records or the replay of past times – resistance to progress.
Rehearsal	Future plans.
Restaurant	Companionship, emotional and physical fulfilment.
River	An emotional need for nurturing. The passage of life. Do you flow with current or swim against it? Each is a message.
Road	The physical direction in life. Is it too narrow, straight, winding, downhill, uphill? The conditions of the road and your attitude to it suggest how you are currently living your life.
Rock	Strength, stability. If blocking the way ahead, it may symbolize an inner block to progress.

Rod	Power, strength, will.
Roof	Mental stability. If in need of repair, we must be still, calm and relaxed to mend it.
Rope	The cord connecting us to the physical body, or our emotional connection with others. If we are tied by the rope, it is limitation, if breaking free, it is expansion.
Sand	Futility (quicksand), lack of foundation.
Satellite	Cosmic communication – maybe from angels, teachers or guides.
Scales	Balance.
Schedule	Restrictions that limit the freedom of expression.
School	Learning. College and university symbolize the Halls of Wisdom and Learning – researching one's own records.
Scissors	*See* Swords.
Seasons	
Spring	New beginnings.
Summer	Completion. The harvesting of seeds sown.
Autumn	Re-evaluation, letting go.
Winter	The end of a cycle.
Secretary	Help needed or given.
Shark	A predator.
Shelf	Putting something on hold.
Shoes	Either the foundation to play various roles in life or, if too many shoes, trying to fill too many roles.
Skeleton	Spiritual deadness.
Sleeping Pills	Escape.
Snail	Slow progress.
Snake	Wisdom, healing, kundalini energy. If coiled, vulnerability. If semi-coiled, head thrust out, the

ability to care for oneself. If elongated, stretched out, healing power, often unrecognized by the dreamer.

Snow	Purity, peace. Frozen conditions.
Speech	Whether listening to or giving a speech it is a message, a teaching, an instruction to express yourself.
Spider	Being trapped by another's power.
Sponge	Absorbing and holding on to emotions, either of self or others.
Stage	One's appearance before others on the stage of life. Initiation to new creativity.
Stairs	The ability to explore higher and lower dimensions of life.
Star	Evolution, expansion, balance of heaven and Earth, the unfolding of personality. Often symbolizes feelings of isolation caused by 'following one's own star'.
Station	Night travel, expansion, movement through different dimensions.
Storm	Emotional eruption.
String	Attachment.
Sun	Communion with God, Christ, life, spiritual energies.
Swan	Spiritual evolution, balance.
Swimming	Exploring and being at ease with the subconscious.
Switch	The power to control.
Sword/Scissors	The power of discrimination, the ability to cut through.
Table	Communication, sharing.
Taxi	Transition.
Telegram	An urgent message from the higher self.

Telephone	Inner, telepathic communication.
Ticket	The freedom to move. If speeding ticket, the need to slow down.
Tie	Emotional/mental connections.
Toilet	Emotional release.
Tower	Foresight, overview.
Train	Flight.
Travel	Expansion.
Trees	The essence of who you are. Look at how firmly grounded and rooted they are. Bare branches imply a stripped feeling; heavily leafed branches, abundance. Branches which reach out mean protection. The weeping willow means depression and the pussy willow, affection and tenderness. The evergreen pine tree, the most psychic of all, symbolizes everlasting life.
Tunnel	Moving through karma.
Umbrella	If open, protection; if closed, unaware of protection.
Uncle	A paternal guardian.
Undressing	The willingness to expose the self to others.
Uniform	Tradition, inflexibility.
University	Soul teaching, spiritual knowledge.
Vegetables	Natural nourishment. (Look at the need for certain nutrients in your diet.)
Vine	The fruits of experience.
Voice	Hearing a voice in a dream usually symbolizes the voice of the teacher.
Waiter/Waitress	The ability to serve.

Wallet	Identity.
Wand	Action, direction.
Watch	*See* Clock.
Water	Spirit or emotions. If clear, purity; if muddy, guilt, lack of clarity.
Weeds	Neglect.
Wheel	Karma, experience; the chakras, the seven vital energy points of the body. *Chakra* means 'wheel' in Sanskrit.
Wind	Cleansing, blowing away the past.
Window	Astral protection.
X-ray	Look within, beyond the surface.
Yawn	Spiritual depletion, draining of energy.
Zoo	One's animal nature restrained.

FURTHER READING

Artemidorus, *Oneicrocritica*, Original Books, 1991

Richard Bach, *Jonathan Livingston Seagull*, Pan, 1973

Alice Bailey, *Discipleship in the New Age*, Lucis Press Trust, 1955

Robert Bauval and Adrian Gilbert, *The Orion Mystery*, Mandarin, 1995

Robert Bauval and Graham Hancock, *Keeper of Genesis*, Mandarin, 1997

Morey Bernstein, *The Search for Bridie Murphy*, Pocket Books, 1978

Dannion Brinkley and Paul Perry, *Saved by the Light*, Piatkus, 1994

—, *Peace in the Light*, Piatkus, 1995

Cicero, *De Divinatione*, Heinemann, 1959

J. W. Dunne, *An Experiment with Time*, Faber, 1939; Macmillan, 1981

Carrington Hereward and Sylvan Muldoon, *The Projection of the Astral Body*, Century, 1989

Ann Ree Colton, *Watch Your Dreams*, ARC Publishing, 1979

Gayle Delaney, *Breakthrough Dreaming*, Bantam, 1997

Jim Gallagher, *The Pierced Priest*, Fount, 1995

Graham Hancock, *Fingerprints of the Gods*, Mandarin, 1996

J. Allan Hobson, *The Dreaming Brain*, Penguin, 1990

David Hoffman, *The Holistic Herbal*, Element Books, 1988
Soozi Holbeche, *The Power of Gems and Crystals*, Piatkus, 1989
—, *The Power of your Dreams*, Piatkus, 1991
—, *Journeys Through Time*, Piatkus, 1995
—, *Changes*, Piatkus, 1997
C. G. Jung, *The Undiscovered Self*, The Princeton University Press, 1990
—, *Man and his Symbols*, Pan, 1978
Christopher Knight and Robert Lomas, *The Hiram Key: Pharaohs, Freemasons and the Discovery of the Secret Scrolls of Jesus*, Arrow Books, 1997
Barbara Marciniak, *Bringers of the Dawn*, Bear and Co., 1993
Kenneth Meadows, *The Medicine Way*, Element Books, 1990
Thomas de Quincey, *Confessions of an English Opium Eater*, 1822
Baird T. Spalding, *The Masters of the Far East*, De Vorss & Co., 1924
Robert Temple, *The Sirius Mystery*, Century, 1998
Erla van Waveren, *Pilgrimage to Rebirth*, Samuel Weiser, 1991
Yogananda, Paramhansa, *Autobiography of a Yogi*, Rider, 1946

INDEX